RICH & DELICIOUS,
LOW CALORIE,
FIGURE SLIMMING
COOKBOOK

By June Roth

THE FREEZE AND PLEASE HOME FREEZER COOKBOOK

RICH & DELICIOUS,

LOW CALORIE,

Figure
Slimming
Cookbook

by

June Roth

Castle Books, New York

ACKNOWLEDGMENTS

The outstanding cooperation of a large group of leading dietetic food manufacturers made the necessary research work on this book a satisfying experience. My requests were met with an avalanche of products for kitchen testing of recipes; tours through factories; and many conferences in person, by phone, and by mail. Letters of permission to use brand names were graciously offered to make sure each recipe could be duplicated exactly by the low-calorie cook.

My sincere and grateful thanks for their patience and valued assistance go to: Sara Hervey Watts, Abbott Laboratories; Ruth L. Rigler, Adolph's Ltd.; Gene Stokes, Chicken of the Sea; Joseph Haims, Clayco Foods Inc.; J. E. Metzger, Dannon Milk Products Inc.; Dr. Saul Blumenthal and Ron Kalmore, Dietetic Food Co. Inc.; Robert D. Jones, Duffy-Mott Co. Pratt-Low Division; Rochelle Walton, General Foods Kitchens; Mary Hale Martin, Libby McNeill & Libby; Richard Kreiss, Loeb Dietetic Food Co.; Sidney B. Ruderman, Louis Sherry Preserves Inc.; Ruth Bakalar and Anne Seltzer, Mott's Figure Control Foods; Janet Taylor, Ocean Spray Cranberries Inc.; Linda Curtis, S & W Fine Foods Inc.; and Marjorie Zimmerman, Stokely-Van Camp Inc.

My deep appreciation is also extended to Herbert Mordana for his editorial advice, Eugene Schwartz for his inspiration, Frederick Fell for his confidence, and to my dear family for their constant encouragement and taste-testing performances during the preparation of this manuscript.

And to a world of hungry weight-watchers, who made this book necessary, go my best wishes for discovering new horizons in eating pleasure.

June Roth

FOREWORD

Watching your weight?

What did you have for dinner yesterday?

Relaxed with a martini first? Only one? It was worth 208 calories after a tiring day. Wish I had joined you.

How about your first course? Cream of mushroom soup . . . a cup instead of a bowl? That's sensible . . . it cuts the soup down to a mere 200 calories. And you had two baking powder biscuits with a pat of butter each? Oh, you used margarine . . . no calorie difference, you know . . . still 50 calories per pat! And the biscuits averaged 130 calories each.

You made up for the first course by having sliced sirloin roast. Two slices? . . . That was 330 calories a slice. What did you have with it?

Peas with a pat of butter . . . nourishing vegetable peas . . . only 170 calories for a cup of the canned variety, and throw in an extra 50 for the butter, please.

Just love French fries, huh? So do I! Had about twenty sticks . . . mmmmm . . . dunked in two tablespoons of ketchup. Sounds good for another 310 calories, plus 50 for the ketchup.

Glad you had a salad with it. What kind of dressing? Thousand Island? I love that too! How much dressing was on the salad . . . about three tablespoons? . . . at 75 calories each? Well, the lettuce was only 20 calories, so it balances out.

Choosing dessert can be a problem. What did you have?

Cherry pie? Oh, you figured that fruit is satisfying and who needs fussy cakes? Nice simple dessert . . . cherry pie . . . add 340 calories.

You weakened and had it a la mode? Yummmmmm . . . add 145 calories more . . . sounds delicious!

Cream and sugar in your coffee? Add 15 for the teaspoon of sugar and 35 more for a tablespoon of light cream.

For just a bit over 3,000 calories, you certainly had a lovely little dinner. The only thing that worries me though is . . . what do you eat when you are not watching your weight?

Now, suppose you skip that martini and have a cup of dietetic cream of mushroom soup for 40 calories. Then dine on dietetic beef slices in barbecue sauce at 128 calories per serving. (Doubled, it is only 256 calories.) Choose a lower calorie vegetable, such as green beans at 15 calories per serving, and substitute another low calorie vegetable, such as carrots for 20 calories per serving (instead of the French fries).

Use a dietetic dressing on your salad for under 10 calories per tablespoon. And top it off with a dietetic chocolate gelatin dessert at 57 calories per serving.

As a bonus, nibble on two 7 calorie tea cookies with your Sucaryl sweetened coffee, and omit the cream, please.

You have now dined tastily on 432 calories, and are well on your way to maintaining your good health while you deplete some of your fat reserve.

No one enjoys a weight-reduction diet which offers only dull starvation portions. This is not necessary, if you revise your cooking to include the use of low-calorie and even no-calorie ingredients. Luckily there are products available that will help you to keep in step with this sensible trend toward low-calorie cooking.

The recipes in this book have been studiously prepared to meet the challenge for streamlined versions of calorie-rich recipes, and yet not lose the recipe's basic appetite appeal. They are low in carbohydrates and fats, and high in protein.

The delicious results are deceptive though . . . you'll be amazed to discover that nothing but calories have been subtracted from many of your favorite dishes!

JUNE ROTH

CONTENTS

With loving gratitude to my mother for her inspiration, and to my daughter Nancy, for continuing the heritage of cooking with care.

An all time favorite: Creamy, rich Baked Custard may now be enjoyed by calorie-counters when it is made with Granulated Sugar Substitute. Smooth eating for a smooth figure!

These hot seafood dishes, Shrimp & Scallop Escabeche, Shrimp Marinara, and Spinach-Cheese Fillets, will tempt the palates of the most meticulous gourmets. So low in calories too!

These calorie-controlled meat dishes in savory sauces are transformed from modern canned food into exciting main dishes, all with rich flavor that belies their low-calorie count.

Hot and hearty Baked Ham and Fruit Salad makes a sunshiny main course; Hot Potato Salad is a surprise bonus for weight-watchers; Savory Green Beans may be served as salad or vegetable. Low-calorie salad dressings make all three salads taste better at less than half the calorie cost of regular dressings.

Slim away with this shimmering Grapefruit-Orange Chiffon Pie. Low-calorie whipped topping and orange garnish promise a rich treat at low cost to your calorie budget. Serves 6 happy people, and so easy to make, too!

New calorie-controlled fruits and toppings make these elegant desserts so low in calories, you can enjoy them in place of regular desserts, and control weight too. No need for a special diet, with dishes like Cold Apricot Souffle, Fruited Meringues, and Chocolate Creme.

Here are tender, delicate sponge-cake rolls, lavished with fine-flavored jellies and preserves, luscious cherries in sauce, even with rich chocolate cream filling. All are yours from 116 to 129 calories a serving. Party food can be fun even when everybody's counting calories!

Brandy-flavored Coffee Eggnog Pie, garnished with low-calorie whipped topping, will strengthen the will of the most wavering dieter. Just too good to be truly low-calorie, but it is!

Now youngsters can have the sweets they crave without sugar, thanks to these tempting, nutty-fruit flavored Apple, Apricot and Grape Bon-Bonnettes, made with Granulated Sugar Substitute. Make a jar full!

For coffee-lovers and calorie-counters, here is a sugar-free and calorie-shy Coffee Sponge Cake. Feather light and easy on the dieter's conscience!

No need to give up cheesecake. This Baked Lemon Cheesecake is an exciting low-calorie replacement for this usually forbidden diet treat. Live in luxury!

Delectable Low Sodium Herb Bread and its exciting variations: Swirl Bread, French Braid Bread, Cocktail Loaf, Quick Cloverleafs, Parker House Rolls, Herb Sticks and Dinner Braids. Seasoned Salt Substitute is the secret of this bread's remarkably low sodium content and provocative flavor.

For a wintertime coffee break, warm up before a cosy fire with a pot of steaming coffee and slices of warm and fragrant Cherry-Nut Bread. Cooperatively low-calorie despite its lingering flavor.

For a holiday breakfast special, bake a homey and heart-warmingly good loaf of Casserole Raisin Bread. Try it sliced and toasted, too. Delicious and deceptively low in calorie count!

A glamour dessert, Chocolate Cheese Loaf is designed to grace-
fully satisfy a chocolate-loving sweet tooth. Looks beautiful and
the calorie count is oh-so-low!

Here is a calorie-controlled paella, tossed green salad with
French-style dressing, pear halves with chocolate topping. The
total calories for the whole meal are the same as those in a glass
of diet formula drink. Only ten minutes to prepare!

RICH & DELICIOUS,
LOW CALORIE,
FIGURE SLIMMING
COOKBOOK

Chapter One

SLIM SENTIMENTS

What is so great about having a slim trim figure?
Everything!
You feel better!
You look better!
You come alive with the youthful vitality that belongs to the unencumbered, fat-free, physically fit who have released themselves from the bondage of dragging sluggish excess poundage through their daily routine.

The waddle becomes a graceful stride. No longer is one confronted with scheming and maneuvering to hide the telltale fatty bulges that threaten to divulge the secret of the overeating overweight.

Buttons rest comfortably in their niches, rather than straining to explode at the very next swallow. Double chins and swollen jowls melt away to reveal youthful facial contours. The illusion of added age disappears as the ever elastic skin firms into place and glows with the inner beauty of good health.

How can you achieve this ideal state of trim allure when you just love good food?

Have you tried reducing pills, only to become nervous and

1

irritable . . . thinking of FOOD the entire time? And did you find that when you stopped the pills, the old eating patterns took over again and the weight crept up to pre-pill plumpness?

Have you tried the high protein diets that blast off the bulges, only to find that you must cheat more often to achieve the emotional satisfaction that emanates from a fancy dessert or a forbidden sweet?

Have you tried monotonous diets . . . and found that was just what they really were? MONOTONOUS! A person might really lose his appetite facing the same dreary fare every day, and with the loss of appetite goes a certain loss of spirit, a loss of emotional fulfillment that comes from supping of gracious foods.

How much cottage cheese and rabbit food does one have to consume before throwing in the sponge and regressing to meals that tempt the palate, and give satisfaction to the business of dining?

How many times have you wished that manufacturers would just TAKE THE CALORIES OUT OF FOOD and let us indulge our need for bulk and variety in our quest for creative sustenance?

Do you know that hundreds of manufacturers are doing just that, right now?

They are busily loading your grocer's shelves with specially prepared low-calorie food products, not as a poor tasting substitute for the foods you normally eat, but as a most appealing assortment of easy to heat and serve foods.

The dietetic food business has become one of the largest growing industries in the United States. Once lumped together on the shelves with many health and fad foods, now the low-calorie products are consuming larger amounts of shelf space in local markets as the widening variety of foods becomes available.

How marvelous to be able to eat chicken à la king, meatballs and spaghetti, mayonnaise, maple syrup, chocolate pudding, Newburg sauce, or Welsh rarebit. This is a dieter's dream come true!

These products are full of the valuable protein, vitamins and minerals you need, but have been reduced in extra fats and sugars that add needless calories which help create over-weight problems.

Naturally, the use of leaner cuts of meat in the meatballs, stews, and sliced beef meals, plus the cost of processing many of these new products with specially devised techniques, results in a higher price than their comparatively higher calorie canned foods. Food chemists work hard and imaginatively to build in taste with the use of vegetables, herbs, spices, and wines. When you consider the additional costs of special materials and new processing, it is surprising to note the small per cent of difference in price that the manufacturers have been able to maintain.

It is wise to take the time to compare the calorie count of each low-calorie product with its regular caloried counterpart, to be sure that the statement on the label of "low-calorie" is not an exaggerated claim, and will indeed give you the benefit you seek. Also note that many of these products are labeled "artificially sweetened" or "packed in water, no salt added, no sugar," and select these on the basis of taste preference. Special dietary problems for diabetic and low-sodium consumers should be resolved under a doctor's care. He will direct you toward the products most suitable for your needs.

Now almost every canned food product has its dietetic competitor. Low-calorie beverage sales have zoomed past thirty million cases in the past year, proving that people are aware of the 10 calories per 8-ounce glass of Cola type soda. Improved taste chemistry has removed the offensive aftertaste that plagued manufacturers in the beginning, and consumers have rewarded their perseverance, in presenting a drink that was pleasant to the palate, by steadily sending the sales of these beverages spiraling up every year.

By taking the calories out of food, the manufacturers have given the chronic dieter some hope for lasting success! Many years of diet dilemmas should prove that there is no cure for overweight, but there is a way to control your weight without resorting to dangerous fad diets, or sporadic starvation.

Advanced research has come to the aid of its weight-watching countrymen and here at last is the answer to dull dieting!

These foods are similar to their higher calorie counter-parts and help to provide a familiar taste experience for your normal meal patterns, while automatically lowering your caloric intake. You can dine on attractive, appealing foods and lose weight comfortably and consistently. You can maintain your interest in meals that have as much variety as the imagination can conceive. You can indulge in a few cookies, a piece or two of low-calorie candy every day, chocolate cream pies, gelatin desserts with whipped toppings, preserves on your toast, and delicious dressings on your salads. If you use these low-calorie products in the same proportion as the foods you normally are accustomed to, you will find that your caloric intake will be less than half.

I have carefully analyzed, tested, and selected outstanding recipes provided by many manufacturers of low-calorie foods for the use of their products. I have also kitchen-tested many combinations of these products, developing from my own expe-rience and love of really fine food. These are all included in the recipe sections and are designed to give you many happy low-caloried meals with freedom from the usual boredom of dieting.

Now your will power need no longer be directed to the refusal of tempting foods, but instead at the acquisition and persistent use of low-calorie foods. By planning especially attrac-tive dishes made with dietetic products for each meal, you will be able to look forward to satisfying your discriminating taste buds and at the same time substantially cut down your caloric intake. This sensible approach to reducing, eliminates the need to search for food fads and miracles. It turns wishful thinkers into long-range "THINK THIN" advocates.

Chapter Two

COMPARING CALORIES

The last ten years might well be described as the Diet Decade in the United States. A recent survey shows that over one hundred million people are weight-conscious, sixty million are overweight, two million are diabetic, a half million mothers-to-be are watching their diets, and over sixteen million people are actually dieting.

It is understandable that every supermarket opened since 1958 has a diet food section, and that 98 per cent of all supermarkets, doing over a million dollars worth of sales a year, now have diet food sections.

The interesting thing about studying low-calorie foods is the actual comparison of these products to their regular food counterparts. Since the high quality protein main dishes are prepared with specially selected low fat meats, and are processed to remove all possible fat, it is understandable that the calorie count is substantially reduced. Cream sauces and cheese sauces are made with a high proportion of non-fat milk solids. Fruit and juices are canned with no sugar, and a non-caloric sweetener only when needed. Salad dressings are low in oil and contain non-caloric vegetable colloids.

The sugar substitutes used have intense sweetening power. A 1-pound sack of saccharine has the sweetening power of 350 pounds of sugar. One pound of calcium cyclamate is equal to 30 pounds of sugar. One is quick to realize that a little sugar substitute goes a long way.

Many manufacturers use a cellulose filler to give bulk to a product, and yet this inert material passes through the body unmetabolized and has no known nutritional value. The bulk is necessary to keep the body satisfied and functioning, and the cellulose is of a similar construction to that found in celery. It might amuse you to know that although a stalk of celery has several calories, it takes more calories to chew the celery than that which it contains. So it is actually a minus-calorie vegetable in its raw state, after being chewed.

Gum arabic used in many candies has non-nutritive value also, and yet serves a function by providing bulk and chewability to many low-calorie treats.

Leading manufacturers of fine foods have recognized the urgent need for low-calorie foods that are high in taste appeal. Test kitchens, nutrition experts, food chemists and intense research combine with studies by leading universities to produce a cross-country presentation of excellent products. These manufacturers deserve your applause for their continuing efforts to improve the fare of the weight-watching public.

On your grocer's shelves you will find meatballs in brown gravy that equal 96 calories, as opposed to 320 calories of regular food. Beef slices in barbecue sauce have 128 calories, against 305. Chicken cacciatore has 76, against 300. Tuna Newburg has 88, against 230. Braised beef and vegetables have 113 calories, against 234.

You can find salad dressings that are delicious and a fraction of their regular caloried counterparts. One tablespoon of French dressing is 10 calories, as opposed to 60 of regular similar dressing. Italian-style dressing is 7 calories, against 63. Bleu cheese dressing is 8 calories against 99. Newburg sauce is 7 calories, against 50. Welsh rarebit is 9 calories, against 48. White sauce is 8 calories, against 28. Spaghetti sauce is 8 calories per tablespoon, against 20. Jellied apple cranberry sauce is 6 calories, against 34.

Sweet syrups are also available in low-calorie form. Chocolate syrup can be found as having 2 calories per teaspoon, against 15. Maple flavored syrup has 1½ calóries per teaspoon, against 20. Flavored syrups that can be added to water or carbonated water to make a refreshing drink, contain no calories whatsoever.

The low-calorie beverage industry accounts for half the sales in the dietetic food departments. Every imaginable flavor is available, containing a negligible number of calories, against about 100 of regular sodas.

While writing this, I am nibbling on a cone-shaped candy in assorted flavors of orange, lemon, raspberry, licorice and peppermint, with approximately 1 calorie per candy. You can get a mouthful of flavor and only a fraction of calories that are found in ordinary candy. They taste remarkably good too!

Preserves are available in every flavor and have from 3 to 9 calories per tablespoon, depending on the brand, against about 55 of the regular variety.

A leading packer of tuna fish offers a dietetic pack of tuna, of white albacore, selected for natural high protein, low fat and sodium content. It is pressure-baked, then packed in water seasoned with low-sodium vegetables. No salt is added. Quality control assures uniform values and the flavor is excellent. A serving contains about 80 calories, against 170 of regular tuna packed in oil.

Mayonnaise, which is regularly 110 calories per tablespoon, can be had in dietetic brands at 15 calories per tablespoon. Whipped dressings have about 10 calories per tablespoon.

Many companies offer excellent gelatin substitutes with calories averaging 10 calories per serving, against 80 for regular gelatin.

Fruits and vegetables are available in a water pack with sugar substitute added when necessary. The vegetables differ only in sodium content, while the fruits average up to half the amount of calories less than do regular products of the same items.

There is an excellent group of canned condensed soups, which includes dietetic pea soup at 49 calories per cup, against 140 of the regular variety. Cream of mushroom soup can be had for 40 calories per cup, against 200. Tomato soup has 37, against 90. Chicken broth averages only a few calories per cup, whether in regular or dietetic pack.

An apple pie filling has 20 calories per ounce, against 58, and a cherry pie filling has 20, against 60.

For ice cream toppings, you can find a chocolate topping at 8 calories per tablespoon, against 63, and a pineapple topping at 9 calories per tablespoon, against 58.

There is a chocolate gelatin custard dessert that has 57 calories per three ounces, against 215 calories, and a vanilla gelatin custard dessert that has 51 calories per three ounce serving, against 113.

All kinds of tea cookies are available at 7 to 32 calories per cookie, to provide a choice of flavorful low-calorie snacks.

Besides an excellent sugar substitute, the leading manufacturer of meat tenderizer has a complete line of low-sodium seasonings which include both the seasoned and unseasoned meat tenderizer, seasoned and unseasoned salt substitute, garlic salt substitute, and onion salt substitute. These are a boon to those restricted by their doctors to a low-sodium diet.

Remember that a diet that is low in calories should be nutritionally adequate. The requirements for protein, vitamins and minerals must be fully met, despite the plan to reduce body weight. With care, it is possible to formulate diet plans which provide from 1,200 to 1,500 calories daily, and which at the same time meet in all respects the requirements of the recommended dietary allowances of the Food and Nutrition Board.

Because the extra calories you consume are stored as fat, to reduce weight it is necessary to consume a diet which forces the body to draw upon its calorie reserves. Your doctor can help you to plan the correct number of calories necessary for you to consume while losing weight pleasantly.

Statistics show that the life-span of overweight adults is less than the life-span of persons whose weights are normal. Many diseases which affect older age groups are more prevalent among the overweight, so excess poundage also saddles its owner with accompanying health burdens.

In 1953 the sales of all diet pack products were $25,000,000. Sales rose in 1958 to over $250,000,000 and reached a high of $600,000,000 in 1962. The industry expects this figure to be well over one billion dollars by 1965.

It will be worth your while to go on a label reading spree in your local supermarket or health food store, to see for yourself the vast number of low-calorie, high taste appeal foods that are waiting for your inspection. Do it today!

Chapter Three

FATTY FOIBLES

Somewhere inside those fat padded cells lives the REAL YOU, surrounded by a wall of overworked excuses that block the way to permanent success in weight control.

Most of us are guilty of pretending that we could buckle down and reduce whenever we so desire. We even use various methods of deception to put off the moment of admitting the need for slimming down.

A clever person can arrange things so those moments of truth are spaced as far apart as possible. Using only waist-high mirrors is one way of avoiding the issue. Neck-high bathroom mirrors are even better!

Aside from bathing suit buying time (and then one can always blame the manufacturer for his skimpy cut and his ridiculous styling), one must avoid shopping for clothes with thinner friends. There are psychological edges to be gained when, instead of watching clothes slither into place neatly over well shaped bones, you are treated to the sight of a well padded body being squeezed hopefully into a bulge-resistant size-too-small. By comparison you will feel sylphlike!

I have often thought that a loud gong on the refrigerator

door would do wonders to help refrain an overeater from the constant opening and closing of that door. Some days it seems as if all the forbidden foods for dieters are the only ones that will give any satisfaction, and yet the persistent dieter continues to scrounge around for a piece of celery, a carrot or two, perhaps an apple . . . and while munching on these is dreaming about a dish of ice cream, or a heavenly piece of candy. Eventually when the will power breaks down, after assorted unsatisfying substitutes of unfamiliar food, the frustrated emotions give up and another well intentioned dieter bites the dust.

Starting a diet is a great adventure for most fatties. Like all adventures it requires several weeks of planning to get accustomed to the idea. The fatty has his own way of packing in preparation for the period of self-denial ahead. He packs in all the food he can consume, excusing his fueling up by the logical reasoning that it won't matter once the great diet begins. Meanwhile he has added several pounds to the pack of fat he is doomed to drag around. Naturally his self-disgust rate rises and his food pacifying continues at an alarming rate, until he finally reaches D-DAY.

Start the moment the truth strikes and you realize the need to reduce your weight, and you will avoid the fatty's packing period. There is no advantage to encumbering yourself with an additional burden. D-DAY is now!

Procrastinating weight collectors are full of tiny trickeries which harm no one but themselves. It is so easy to pretend that we are seriously dieting, and that one slip won't matter very much in the final outcome. And in truth it won't. What will matter will be the sum of all the calorie cheating throughout each week as we secretly yield to our innate desire to be sociable or to pacify our emotions.

There are roughly 3,500 calories in each stored pound of fat on your body. You can lose that 1 pound a week by eating 500 calories less each day. To lose 2 pounds a week, you would have to eat 1,000 calories less each day than your present caloric consumption. Dietetic foods have the fat largely removed, while maintaining high protein, vitamin rich main dishes. It is not difficult to save 1,000 calories a day by using these specially prepared low-calorie foods.

In order to pare pounds off happily while substituting low calorie foods, try to acquire dining tricks that will make your dieting a pleasant experience. Taking the time to serve food attractively pays dividends. A lettuce leaf slipped under a salad, a strip of pimento for just the right accent, a slice of dill pickle, a dash of paprika, a sliver of lemon, or a garnish of parsley, all help to signify that this platter has received loving care in its preparation. Just because someone is on a diet is no reason to assume that he has given up the pleasure and enjoyment of mealtime. Weight control will not have much success unless it is accompanied by satisfying meals that look and taste good.

Longer mealtimes play an important role in the emotional satisfaction of eating. One way to prolong the meal is to develop the habit of eating slowly. Deliberately at first, reduce your speed to a slow motion facsimile of your usual dining gusto. Put less on each forkful. Break your bread into smaller pieces, and linger over the process of spreading the bread with a low calorie substitute. Cutting a sandwich in four parts instead of two, will give the illusion of more to eat. Dragging the actual eating time out will prove to be more relaxing and more satisfying an experience than gulping food down quickly, only to leave the table hungry.

Another trick is to break your meal down into as many courses on as many plates as possible. This also gives the illusion of more to eat, while the caloric intake is regulated by pre-planning.

This theory is probably based on the same one taught to new mothers about feeding their babies. Even if a baby could digest its feeding twice as fast, it should not be deprived of the instinctive need for a longer feeding period to keep itself tranquil and comfortable.

If you are a dinner guest at someone's home, try not to announce that you are dieting. Some hostesses are offended by the statement, and are challenged into urging you to give up the idea, just for tonight. It is far wiser to keep your diet a secret, and to eat around the offered food. By eating around it, I refer to the process of starting the course with everyone else, but if you cannot afford the calories, just eat some and spread the rest around the plate with no apologies. That way, everyone will be too busy to inspect just how much of the proffered course you have consumed. Surely you do not need attention badly enough to become the center of conversation and the object of all the invisible calorie calculating machines that will spring into action the moment you mention your diet. Your amount of consumption is indeed your private affair, and you will be able to enjoy this innocent deception when your thinner figure becomes more apparent. At any rate there is nothing more devastating to a well planned dinner party than the topic of dieting, as the guilt complexes are sure to multiply and ruin your hostess's favorite dessert.

A dieter's theme song should be, "Never do today what you can put off until tomorrow." Doctors seem to agree that it is decidedly unhealthy continually to fluctuate your weight between sporadic dieting and overeating. Therefore, it would be wiser to analyze your attitude toward food and dieting, and to plan a long-range change that realistically includes your love of good tasting meals and your need for variety. Dietetic foods offer you this challenge to change your brands of foods and not your way of eating. By TAKING THE CALORIES OUT OF THE FOOD, they offer you the opportunity to dine comfortably and diet effectively at the same time.

Chapter Four

TEMPTING TIDBITS

People who have to diet are the people who love to eat, and people who love to eat won't put up too long with stingy dining.

A tiny attractive first course, low in calories but high in visual and taste appeal, does much to help the dieter follow his determined program to reduce. Miracle first courses can be devised for 50 calories or less that will take the edge off your appetite. In fact, by stealing these relatively few calories for a starter course, you are insuring the probability of sticking to your diet plan.

By now you must realize that this book is not about how to starve and look greedy-eyed as you compare your skimpy platter to another's sumptuous dinner. It is about how to dine graciously and lose weight consistently on many course meals, low-calorie though they may be.

Therefore, I urge you to consider this first course as a necessary prerequisite to dinner, to sweeten your disposition and encourage your will power. Count your calories, and count on investing a few in a tempting appetizer.

APRICOT-GRAPE COMPOTE

1 (8 ounce) can Pratt-Low Dietetic Apricots
1 (8 ounce) can Pratt-Low Dietetic Seedless Grapes
1 tablespoon grated orange rind
Dash of nutmeg

Combine the apricots and grapes in 4 compotes. Sprinkle with orange rind, and dash of nutmeg.
Serves 4. (53 calories per serving.)

CHERRY-PLUM COMPOTE

1 (8 ounce) can Pratt-Low Dietetic Greengage Plums
1 (8 ounce) can Pratt-Low Dietetic Royal Anne Cherries
3 thin slices lemon, quartered

Divide the plums and cherries into 4 compotes. Garnish with quartered thinly sliced lemon pieces.
Serves 4. (51 calories per serving.)

CHICKEN-LIVER-STUFFED CELERY

1 bunch celery
1 (4½ ounce) can Mott's Figure Control Chopped Chicken Livers

Cut celery stalks in 2-inch lengths, spread about 1 tablespoon chopped chicken livers in each celery length.
16 calories each (51 calories each with regular chopped chicken livers).

CRABMEAT ROYALE

2 cups crabmeat (canned and shredded)
1 cup finely chopped celery
1 teaspoon finely grated onion
3 tablespoons Mott's Figure Control French Dressing
¼ teaspoon curry powder
2 hard-cooked eggs, cut in quarters
¼ cup Mott's Figure Control Whipped Dressing

Mix crabmeat with chopped celery, grated onion and French dressing. Refrigerate. Just before serving add curry powder to the whipped dressing and lightly toss into the crabmeat mixture. Serve on a lettuce cup with a wedge of hard-cooked egg as a garnish.

Serves 8. (59 calories per serving.)

GRAPEFRUIT COUPETTE

1 (8 ounce) can S & W Nutradiet Pack Grapefruit Sections
2 teaspoons Louis Sherry Dietetic Blueberry Preserve

Divide chilled grapefruit sections between 2 compote dishes. Put a teaspoon of dietetic blueberry preserve on the center of each compote.

Serves 2. (37 calories per serving.)

KADOTA FIGS

1 (8 ounce) can Pratt-Low Dietetic Whole Kadota Figs
1 tablespoon raisins
Dash of cinnamon

Divide one can of whole Kadota figs into 3 compotes. Sprinkle with raisins and a dash of cinnamon.

Serves 3. (52 calories per serving.)

MOCK PEACH MELBA

1 (8 ounce) can Pratt-Low Dietetic Peach Halves
4 tablespoons cottage cheese
2 tablespoons Louis Sherry Black Raspberry Dietetic Jelly
4 lettuce cups

Arrange a lettuce cup on each of 4 salad plates. Center a peach half on each, filled with 1 tablespoon of cottage cheese. Drizzle black raspberry dietetic jelly over each stuffed peach half.
Serves 4. (34 calories per serving.)

ORANGE BASKET

3 oranges
1 (8 ounce) can Pratt-Low Dietetic Fruit Cocktail

Cut oranges in half. Scoop out segments and set aside. About ¼ inch down from the top rim of the half orange, cut halfway across. Fold back the cut half of rim and fasten with a toothpick, being careful not to snap the "handle" off. Mix fruit cocktail with the orange segments and refill the baskets.
Serves 6. (45 calories per basket.)

ORANGE DELIGHT

1 orange, peeled and cut in sections
1 (8 ounce) can Pratt-Low Seedless Grapes
½ cup fresh halved strawberries

Combine orange sections and grapes in 4 fruit compotes. Arrange halves of strawberries around the top of each dish.
Serves 4. (57 calories per serving.)

PINEAPPLE-BANANA COMPOTE

1 can Libby's Dietetic Pineapple Tidbits, chilled
1 sliced banana
½ cup fresh orange juice
1 tablespoon grated coconut

Combine dietetic pineapple tidbits and the sliced banana into 4 compote dishes. Pour some orange juice over each. Top with a sprinkling of grated coconut.
Serves 4. (53 calories per serving.)

SHRIMP-PINEAPPLE RINGLET

12 medium cooked shrimps
2 slices Libby's Dietetic Pineapple Rings
4 lettuce cups
1 tablespoon Loeb Dietetic Mayonnaise
1 tablespoon tomato ketchup
Sprigs of parsley

Arrange a ½ slice of pineapple on each lettuce cup. Combine dietetic mayonnaise and ketchup, then mix shrimps, thoroughly coating them with this dressing. Place 3 coated shrimps in the center of each ½ pineapple ring. Garnish with a sprig of parsley.
Serves 4. (52 calories per serving.)

SHRIMP NEWBURG

12 medium shrimps, cooked and peeled
½ cup Mott's Figure Control Newburg Sauce
4 lettuce cups

Heat Newburg sauce, stirring constantly to prevent sticking. Arrange three shrimps on each lettuce cup. Spoon hot sauce over shrimps. Garnish with a dash of paprika and a bit of parsley.
Serves 4. (47 calories per serving.)

SPARKLING FRUIT SALAD

1 (8 ounce) can Pratt-Low Dietetic Fruit Salad, drained
½ cup dietetic ginger ale
1 tablespoon grated orange rind

Divide the fruit salad into two compotes. Pour ¼ cup of dietetic ginger ale over each mound of fruit salad. Top with a sprinkling of grated orange rind.
Serves 2. (44 calories per serving.)

STRAWBERRY GRAPEFRUIT

1 grapefruit, cut in half
2 teaspoons Louis Sherry Dietetic Strawberry Jelly

Carefully cut around the grapefruit segments, loosening them but leaving them in place. Place a dollop of strawberry jelly in the center of each half.
Serves 2. (51 calories per serving.)

TINY TUNA SURPRISE

1 can Chicken-of-the-Sea Brand Dietetic Tuna
18 tiny cherry tomatoes
1 tablespoon Loeb Dietetic Mayonnaise
6 lettuce cups
Dash of paprika

Arrange lettuce cups on six small dishes. Scoop out tiny tomatoes. Mash the tuna with dietetic mayonnaise. Fill each tomato with the tuna mixture. Dash paprika over each for color contrast. Place 3 tomato surprises on each lettuce cup.
Serves 6. (49 calories per serving.)

Chapter Five

SLENDER SOUPS

A blender will be your most valued piece of kitchen equipment when you discover the ease of making your own low-calorie soups in it. If you do not own a blender, a sieve will do.

Almost the first thing every weight-watcher learns is that bouillon, broth, and consommé contain negligibly few calories. Compressed cubes of these soups are made by many manufacturers, and are useful as a hot drink throughout the day. Any diet-pack vegetable with its own liquid can become a low-calorie soup by joining a bouillon cube or two in the blender. Add water to get desired thickness, and add seasonings to taste.

Several dietetic condensed soups are available. Some need the addition of salt to improve the flavor for those who are not restricted to a low-sodium diet. For those who are restricted, there are salt substitutes available in both seasoned and unseasoned forms. These soups are very satisfactory as is, and can be garnished with a bit of parsley, a floating paper-thin notched slice of lemon, or a pinch of a complementary herb. A teaspoon of sherry added to some soups leaves an intriguing flavor, as the calories evaporate during cooking.

Many tried and true recipes are included in this chapter to get you started on your own inventive path.

QUICK ASPARAGUS SOUP

1 (8 ounce) can S & W Nutradiet Asparagus
1 can water
2 bouillon cubes
   Salt to taste

Put asparagus and water into your blender. Blend, then pour into a small saucepan. Add bouillon cubes and heat until cubes have melted. Add salt to taste.
Serves 2. (26 calories per serving.)

CLAM AND TOMATO BISQUE

1 cup canned clam broth
1 (8 ounce) can Claybourne Dietetic Tomato Soup
½ cup skim milk
   Dash of onion salt
   Dash of nutmeg

In a small skillet, blend clam broth into the condensed soup. Add milk. Add a dash of onion salt and a dash of nutmeg. Salt to taste. Serve hot.
Serves 3. (39 calories per serving.)

COLD TOMATO-BEET SOUP

1 (8 ounce) can S & W Nutradiet Sliced Beets, with juice
1 (8 ounce) can Claybourne Condensed Dietetic Tomato Soup
1 soup can of cold water
½ teaspoon salt

Blend the sliced beets and the tomato soup with a soup can of water. Add salt to taste. Serve cold with slice of lemon or diced floating cucumber.
Serves 4. (34 calories per serving.)

QUICK TOMATO SOUP

1 can Mott's Figure Control Vegetable Juice Cocktail
2 bouillon cubes
  Thinly sliced lemon

Heat vegetable juice cocktail with bouillon cubes until cubes are blended. Serve with floating slice of thin lemon. Salt to taste.

Serves 3. (20 calories per serving.)

TOMATO-CHEESE SOUP

1 (12 ounce) can Mott's Figure Control Tomato Soup
½ can (¾ cup) Mott's Figure Control Cheese Rarebit

Heat together.

Serves 3. Only 68 calories per serving (regular has 238).

QUICK BORSCHT

1 (8 ounce) can S & W Nutradiet Beets, chilled
1 tablespoon lemon juice
½ can water
½ teaspoon salt
¼ teaspoon Sucaryl

Blend the above ingredients in your blender. Serve with diced floating cucumber.

Serves 3. (23 calories per serving.)

CRAB MEAT BISQUE

1 (8 ounce) can Claybourne Dietetic Pea Soup
1 (8 ounce) can Claybourne Dietetic Tomato Soup
6½ ounce can crab meat, flaked
½ teaspoon salt
2 tablespoons sherry
1 cup skim milk

Blend the skim milk into the condensed pea soup and tomato soup. Add salt and sherry. Simmer for 5 minutes. Add crab meat and simmer for another 5 minutes. Serve hot at once.
Serves 6. (76 calories per serving.)

LOBSTER BISQUE

½ cup diced lobster meat (cooked or canned)
1 (8 ounce) can Claybourne Dietetic Cream of Mushroom Soup
1 tablespoon sherry
1 cup skim milk
Salt and pepper to taste

Blend the milk and sherry into the condensed soup. Add diced lobster meat. Season to taste. Add a dash of paprika to each bowlful for color.
Serves 3. (74 calories per serving.)

QUICK FISH CHOWDER

1 (8 ounce) can Claybourne Dietetic Vegetable Soup
1 cup tomato juice
1 cup flaked, cooked haddock
½ teaspoon salt
¼ teaspoon pepper

In a small skillet, blend the tomato juice into the condensed soup. Add flaked fish. Add salt and pepper. Heat and serve hot.
Serves 3. (66 calories per serving.)

FRENCH ONION SOUP

2 cups thinly sliced large onions
2 (8 ounce) cans Claybourne Dietetic Chicken Broth, diluted
1 teaspoon salt

¼ teaspoon pepper
1 slice toast
2 tablespoons grated parmesan cheese
1 tablespoon butter

Saute onions in butter until golden. Add broth, salt and pepper, and simmer with cover on for a half hour. Serve with ¼ slice toast, sprinkled with grated parmesan cheese.

Serves 4. (83 calories per serving.)

GAZPACHO

2 cans Mott's Figure Control Tomato Soup
1 cup thinly sliced cucumber
½ cup finely chopped green pepper
¼ cup freshly minced onion

¼ cup Mott's Figure Control Italian dressing
1 small garlic clove
¼ teaspoon salt
Dash of tabasco

Combine all ingredients. Cover and refrigerate at least 4 hours. Stir gently. Serve chilled, with lemon or lime slice.

Serves 8. (36 calories per serving.)

PEA SOUP AUX CROUTONS

1 can water
1 (8 ounce) can Claybourne Pea Soup
1 (8 ounce) can Claybourne Chicken Broth
½ teaspoon salt
16 croutons

Blend the pea soup and chicken broth together with 1 can of water. Add salt. Heat. Serve in a cup, topped with 4 floating croutons.

Serves 4. (31 calories per serving.)

QUICK PEA SOUP

1 (8 ounce) can S & W Nutradiet Peas
1 bouillon cube
1 can water

1 pinch dried tarragon
1 pinch mace
½ cup dry white wine

Blend peas and water in an electric blender until smooth. Pour into small saucepan and add the bouillon cube. Add tarragon and mace. Add white wine. Simmer until bouillon cube has melted. Serve hot.

Serves 3. (32 calories per serving.)

SPINACH SOUP

1 package frozen chopped spinach, thawed
2 (8 ounce) cans Claybourne
Dietetic Chicken Broth

1 tablespoon finely minced
onion
⅛ teaspoon pepper
1 teaspoon salt
¼ teaspoon nutmeg

Put thawed spinach into your blender. Add 1 can of dietetic chicken broth. Blend. Pour into a saucepan and add the second can of chicken broth. Add onion, pepper, salt, and nutmeg. Simmer for 20 minutes.

Serves 6. (25 calories per serving.)

Chapter Six

ENTICING ENTREES

Like Scheherazade telling a story for a thousand and one *Arabian Nights,* to maintain the king's interest and thus save her life, the dietetic meal planner must use every means to keep meals versatile and satisfying.

With the amazing array of meats, poultry and fish available in markets today, plus new tricks with low-calorie canned products, it indeed might be possible to spend a thousand and one nights without repeating the same dinner menu over again.

Simple broiled, stewed and roasted meats contain the least calories. Cooking fats vary from 100 calories per tablespoon of butter, to 125 calories per tablespoon of cooking oil, and up to 135 calories per tablespoon of lard. By eliminating fried foods, you avoid hundreds of unneeded calories from prepared meat dishes.

Broiled meats will grow less tiresome when you vary the flavor and slip dietetic fruits under the broiler to add a surprise touch to an otherwise routine platter. Often a single addition spread on simply prepared meats will create a new special taste treat.

By using prepared dietetic sauces, you will be able to indulge in the type of entrees that are usually forbidden to dieters. These creamed dishes are calorie controlled to give a minimum of calories for a maximum of taste.

It is of utmost importance to maintain an interesting variety of main courses to permit the dieter continually to adventure down gustatory avenues. Dieting does not have to be dull . . . try some of these recipes and prove it to yourself!

CRAB NEWBURG

1 can Mott's Figure Control Newburg Sauce
2 cans flaked canned king crab meat
1/8 teaspoon nutmeg
1/4 teaspoon dried thyme
1 tablespoon cooking sherry

Add nutmeg, thyme, and cooking sherry to the Newburg sauce. Simmer and stir for 5 minutes. Add flaked crab meat. Heat another few minutes, then serve on toast points.

Serves 4. (139 calories per serving.)

BAKED FISH WITH SPAGHETTI SAUCE

1 (12 ounce) package frozen fish fillets, of flounder, partially thawed
1 small thin sliced onion
1/2 clove minced garlic
8 ounces Mott's Figure Control Spaghetti Sauce
1 tablespoon parsley flakes

Arrange fish in a shallow baking pan. Spread thin onion slices over the fish. Sprinkle with finely minced garlic. Top with spaghetti sauce. Bake in a 400-degree oven for 25 minutes. Garnish with sprinkled parsley flakes.

Serves 3. (111 calories per serving.)

FILLETS NEWBURG

1½ pounds fillet of flounder
 1 can Mott's Figure Control Low-calorie Newburg Sauce
 2 tablespoons grated parmesan cheese

Arrange fillets flat in a baking dish. Pour Newburg sauce over the top. Sprinkle with grated parmesan cheese. Add a few dashes of paprika. Bake uncovered at 350 degrees for about 30 minutes, or until fish flakes easily with a fork but is still moist.

Serves 4. (170 calories per serving.)

SHRIMP MARINARA

3 pounds fresh shrimp
1 cup Mott's Figure Control Spaghetti Sauce

Peel and devein shrimp. Bring sauce to a boil in a saucepan; add shrimp, simmer 2 to 5 minutes or until tender. Garnish with parsley and lemon wedges.

Serves 8. (119 calories per serving.)

GARLIC BROILED SHRIMPS

2 pounds large raw shrimps, deveined and peeled
½ teaspoon salt
½ teaspoon paprika
1 tablespoon dried parsley flakes
2 tablespoons butter
1 crushed garlic clove

In a small saucepan, melt butter and add remaining seasonings. Remove from heat. Arrange shrimps on a flat broiling pan. With a pastry brush, coat the shrimps with the butter mixture. Broil for 6 minutes, turn and broil 6 minutes more. Serve hot. Serves 4. About 150 calories per serving.

SHRIMP AND SCALLOP ESCABECHE

3 pounds fresh shrimp
¾ pound scallops
1 medium red onion, sliced thinly
1 bottle (8 oz.) Mott's Figure Control Italian Dressing

Peel and devein shrimp. Bring water to a boil, add shrimp and scallops; simmer 2 to 5 minutes, or until pink and tender. Drain. Combine shrimp, scallops and sliced onion rings. Pour Italian dressing over, cover and refrigerate several hours, or overnight.
Serves 12. (108 calories per serving.)

SEAFOOD AU GRATIN

1 cup crab meat or diced lobster, cooked or canned
1 (8 ounce) can Claybourne Dietetic Concentrated Cream of Mushroom Soup
1 tablespoon parmesan cheese
1 tablespoon sherry
½ teaspoon salt
¼ teaspoon pepper

Blend the sherry and parmesan cheese into the undiluted soup. Season with salt and pepper. Add diced seafood. Bake in a 350-degree oven for 20 minutes. Serve hot.
Serves 2. (140 calories per serving.)

SPINACH-CHEESE FILLETS

1½ pounds fillet of flounder
1 package (10 ounce) frozen chopped spinach, thawed
1 can Mott's Figure Control Welsh Rarebit

Fold fillets in half, lengthwise. Roll and fasten with picks or skewers. Fill centers with spinach. Arrange in a baking dish and pour Welsh rarebit over. Bake uncovered at 350 degrees F. for about 30 minutes, or until fish flakes easily with fork but is still moist.

Serves 4. (189 calories per serving) (with regular Welsh rarebit, 423 calories per serving).

STUFFED PEPPER CUPS

2 cans Mott's Figure Control Tuna Newburg
6 medium green peppers

Cut off pepper tops. Scoop out seeds and membranes. Spoon ½ cup Tuna Newburg into each pepper cup. Bake in a shallow dish with water just to cover the bottom, in a 350-degree oven for about 20 minutes.

Stuffed peppers are 103 calories each (would be 245 with regular Tuna Newburg).

TUNA ORIENTAL

1 (8 ounce) can Claybourne Dietetic Cream of Mushroom Soup
½ can water
1 can Chicken-of-the-Sea Brand Dietetic Tuna
1 cup chow mein noodles
1 cup sliced celery
1 chopped onion
½ pound sliced fresh mushrooms
1 teaspoon salt

Blend soup and water. Add tuna in broken pieces, noodles, celery, onion and thin sliced fresh mushrooms. Add salt. Bake at 375 degrees in an ungreased flat dish for about 20 minutes. Garnish with mandarin oranges and dietetic pineapple tidbits. Serves 4. (119 calories per serving, without garnish.)

TUNA PUFF

    1 can Mott's Figure Control Tuna Newburg
    2 eggs, separated
    ⅛ teaspoon salt
      Pinch of cayenne

Heat Tuna Newburg and stir in lightly beaten egg yolks and cayenne. Beat egg whites stiffly with salt; fold into tuna mixture. Bake in a 1-quart casserole, 400 degrees F. for about 15 minutes.
Serves 4. (114 calories per serving) (236 calories a serving with regular Tuna Newburg).

TUNA STUFFED TOMATO

3 medium firm tomatoes	2 stalks celery, diced
1 can Chicken-of-the-Sea Brand Dietetic Tuna	2 tablespoons Loeb's Dietetic Mayonnaise
1 small apple, diced	3 lettuce cups

Place each tomato on a lettuce cup. Core, and slice into quarters part way to the bottom.
In a small bowl, mash tuna; add diced apple and diced celery. Mix through with dietetic mayonnaise. Put one-third of the mixture into the center of each tomato. Garnish with cold canned asparagus.
Serves 3. (134 calories per serving, without garnish.)

PAELLA

4 cans (8 oz. each) Mott's Figure Control Chicken Cacciatore
1⅓ cups precooked quick rice
1 can (1 lb. 1 oz.) steamed clams (optional)

Stir uncooked rice and chicken cacciatore together in a skillet or flame-proof casserole. Arrange steamed clams around the edges, if desired. Cover pan and steam 10 minutes, until rice is cooked.

Serves 8. (161 calories each.)

BAKED CHICKEN IN FOIL

1 broiler, quartered
½ cup Mott's Figure Control French Dressing
½ lemon
Silver foil, 4 squares

Rub chicken with the half of lemon. Coat surface with French dressing. Wrap airtight in the silver foil paper. Bake for 1 hour at 350 degrees, or place on outdoor grill, turning after 15 minutes.

Serves 4. (180 calories per serving.)

BAKED CHICKEN WITH PEACH PRESERVE

2 broilers, cut up in pieces
1 bottle Diamel Italian Dressing
¼ cup Diamel Pancake Sweetener
½ cup orange juice
¼ cup Diamel Peach Preserves

Blend the Italian dressing, pancake sweetener, orange juice, and peach preserves into a marinade. Soak cut up pieces of chicken for at least 1 hour in this marinade. Then bake in a flat roasting pan for approximately 1 hour at 350 degrees, basting occasionally with the remaining marinade.

Serves 8. (213 calories per serving.)

CHICKEN DIVAN

1 package frozen broccoli, cooked
2 (8 ounce) cans Claybourne Dietetic Cream of Mushroom Soup, undiluted
1 tablespoon sherry
½ cup skim milk
2 tablespoons grated parmesan cheese
½ teaspoon salt
¼ teaspoon pepper
8 large slices cooked chicken

Arrange cooked broccoli on bottom of a shallow casserole. In a saucepan, blend the mushroom soup, skim milk, sherry, and grated parmesan cheese. Season with salt and pepper. Heat through, stirring constantly. Place chicken slices on top of the broccoli and pour the hot sauce over the chicken. Bake in a 350-degree oven for 20 minutes.

Serves 4. (201 calories per serving.)

QUICK CHICKEN DIVAN

1 package (10 oz.) frozen broccoli spears
3 cans (8 oz. each) Mott's Figure Control Chicken à la King
1 tablespoon grated Parmesan cheese

Arrange frozen broccoli spears in a baking dish, cover with chicken à la king, and sprinkle with Parmesan cheese. Bake in a 350-degree oven until broccoli is tender and topping is golden brown, about 35-45 minutes. Or first simmer broccoli in boiling salted water until it is barely tender, to reduce baking time to 20-25 minutes.

Serves 4. 173 calories per serving. (Regular Chicken Divan has more than 1,000 calories per serving!)

CHICKEN AND MEATBALL STEW

1 can Mott's Figure Control Chicken à la King
1 can Mott's Figure Control Meatballs in Brown Gravy

Combine chicken and meatball dishes. Heat.
Serves 4. 212 calories per serving. (The same dish prepared with regular foods would be 530 calories.)

CHICKEN SALAD RING MOLD

4 1-ounce envelopes Lemon D-Zerta Gelatin
3½ cups hot chicken broth (can be made with bouillon cubes)
1 teaspoon salt
1 teaspoon finely minced onion
4 tablespoons lemon juice
1½ cups cubed fresh tomatoes
½ cup dietetic mayonnaise
2 cups diced cooked chicken
1 cup finely diced celery
2 tablespoons finely minced dill pickle

Dissolve the gelatin in the hot chicken broth, add salt and lemon juice. Add minced onion, and chill until slightly thickened.

Mix remaining ingredients together, and add to chilled gelatin mixture. Blend thoroughly and fill a 2-quart mold with the mixture. Chill until firm. Unmold on crisp salad greens.
Serves 8. (135 calories per serving.)

CHICKEN SALAD SURPRISE

4 cups diced, cooked chicken
1 cup diced celery
1 can Pratt-Low Dietetic Seedless Grapes, drained
½ teaspoon salt
¼ teaspoon pepper
½ cup Loeb dietetic mayonnaise
¼ cup diced pimento
6 lettuce cups

Combine the chicken, celery, and drained grapes. Add pimento, reserving several strips for garnishing. Season with salt and pepper, and blend mayonnaise through thoroughly. Serve on crisp lettuce cups.

Serves 6. (171 calories per serving.)

CHICKEN TANGO

1 3-pound broiler chicken
1 (8 ounce) can Claybourne Dietetic Condensed Tomato Soup
6 sliced black olives

¼ pound fresh sliced mushrooms
1 onion, sliced
1 medium green pepper, diced
1 clove garlic
½ cup red wine

In a large saucepan, blend the tomato soup, olives, pepper, mushrooms, onion, crushed garlic and wine. Immerse whole chicken into this sauce, and simmer covered for 1 hour.

Serves 4. (218 calories per serving.)

CHICKEN-ZUCCHINI CACCIATORE

2 small zucchini squash
2 cans Mott's Figure Control Chicken Cacciatore

Slice zucchini and add to chicken cacciatore. Cook 10 minutes.

Serves 4. (136 calories per serving.) (Regular would have 513 calories.)

PINEAPPLE-BAKED CHICKEN

2 broilers, quartered
1 tablespoon prepared mustard
1 can Libby's Dietetic Pineapple Tidbits

Juice of 1 lemon
1 teaspoon salt
1 teaspoon Adolph's Granulated Sugar Substitute

Arrange pieces of the broilers in a large flat roasting pan, skin side down. Combine the rest of the ingredients and spread half of the mixture over the chicken parts. Bake in a 350-degree oven for 20 minutes and turn chicken parts over. Spread with remaining pineapple mixture. Bake until tender, about another 20 minutes.

Serves 8. (198 calories per serving.)

STUFFED TOMATO CUPS

2 cans Mott's Figure Control Chicken à la King
6 medium tomatoes

Cut zigzag edge around the tops of tomatoes, remove tops. Scoop out tomato meat. Spoon ½ cup chicken à la king into each tomato cup. Bake in a shallow dish with water just to cover the bottom, in a 350-degree oven for about 20 minutes.

Stuffed tomatoes are 106 calories each (would be 318 with regular chicken à la king).

BROILED DUCKLING WITH APRICOT SAUCE

1 duckling, quartered
½ teaspoon salt
1 tablespoon grated lemon rind
2 tablespoons lemon juice

¼ cup Louis Sherry Dietetic Apricot Preserves
Dash of ginger

Place duckling on broiler rack, skin side down, about 5 inches away from flame. As skin browns, prick in several places to release fat. Broil for 35 minutes and turn over. Baste with a mixture of the remaining ingredients, and broil for another 35 minutes, or until done.

Serves 4. (358 calories per serving.)

BAKED HAM AND FRUIT SALAD

½ pound cooked ham, cut in
large chunks (about 1 cup)
1 can (1 lb. 4 oz.) Mott's
Figure Control Pineapple
Rings
1 jar (7½ oz.) Mott's Figure
Control Apricot Halves

1 jar (7½ oz.) Mott's Figure
Control Peach Slices
1 jar (7½ oz.) Mott's Figure
Control Cooked Prunes
2 stalks celery, sliced diagonally
¼ cup Mott's Figure Control
Whipped Dressing

Mix ingredients together, arrange in a shallow baking dish.
Warm in a 350-degree oven for 15 minutes.

Serves 8. 121 calories per serving. (With regular fruits and
dressings, this would be 254 calories per serving.)

GLAZED HAM SLICES

4 ¾-inch slices boned rolled cooked ham
4 tablespoons Mott's Figure Control Apricot-Pineapple Preserves
1 can whole tiny carrots, drained

Arrange ham slices in a flat baking dish. Surround the
ham slices with whole tiny canned carrots. Spread apricot-
pineapple preserves over all. Bake in a 325-degree oven for
40 minutes, or until glazed. Garnish with parsley.

Serves 4. (399 calories per serving.)

BARBECUED LAMB STEAKS

4 lamb steaks, ½-inch thick and lean
½ cup Mott's Figure Control Spaghetti Sauce
1 teaspoon grated onion
½ teaspoon horse-radish
½ teaspoon oregano

Blend grated onion, horse-radish and oregano into the spaghetti sauce. Place lamb steaks in flat baking dish. Spread with barbecue sauce, cover and bake in a 350-degree oven for 30 minutes.

Serves 4. (288 calories per serving.)

BROILED LAMB CHOPS

    6 large shoulder lamb chops
    2 tablespoons Mott's Figure Control Italian Dressing
    6 canned pear halves, drained
      Dash of salt and pepper

Brush the lamb chops with Italian dressing. Broil. Turn over and brush other side with Italian dressing. Add dash of salt and pepper to taste. Arrange 6 pear halves on broiler alongside the chops. Broil until done. Can add a dollop of mint jelly to the pear halves a minute before removing from broiler.

Serves 6. (255 calories per serving.)

LAMB CHOPS WITH BASIL

    4 thick lamb chops, trimmed very lean
    2 teaspoons basil
    1 teaspoon salt
    ⅛ teaspoon pepper
    1 teaspoon lemon rind, grated

Combine the basil, salt, pepper and lemon rind. Sprinkle half the mixture on top of the lamb chops. Broil 10 minutes. Turn and sprinkle remaining seasonings on the other side. Broil until done.

Serves 4. (280 calories per serving.)

ROAST LEG OF LAMB IN MARINADE

1 cup Mott's Figure Control Italian Dressing
1 garlic clove
1 6-pound leg of lamb

Rub leg of lamb with the peeled clove of garlic. Rub dressing over the roast and wrap in aluminum foil. Marinate in this way for several hours, or overnight. Remove from foil and roast in an open pan in a 350-degree oven. Baste frequently with marinade and drippings.

Serves 8. (240 calories per 3 ounce slice.)

BARBEQUED SPARE RIBS

1 rack of spare ribs
1 bottle Diamel Italian Dressing
¼ cup Diamel Pancake Sweetener
½ cup orange juice
¼ cup Diamel Orange Marmalade

Simmer spare ribs in water for about half an hour. Drain water. Blend remaining ingredients above and marinate spare ribs for at least 1 hour. Bake in a 350-degree oven for 1 hour, basting with the remaining marinade.

Serves 6. (278 calories per serving.)

ROAST BEEF SLICES IN WINE GRAVY

1 can Mott's Figure Control Low-calorie Roast Beef Slices
¼ cup red wine (not sweet)
Salt to taste

Add wine to the roast beef slices and gravy. Salt to taste. Simmer gently so that wine evaporates, leaving only the flavor. Can serve on rice, gluten noodles, or a slice of toast. Serves 4. 128 calories per serving.

SHOULDER OF VEAL ROAST WITH SAUERKRAUT

2-pound boned shoulder of veal, rolled and tied
2 onions, sliced thin
1 clove minced garlic
1 tablespoon salt

1 can condensed beef bouillon, or equivalent in diluted bouillon cubes
3 teaspoons paprika
1 can Stokely's Finest Sauerkraut, drained
1 teaspoon caraway seeds

In a Dutch oven, or large heavy covered pot, combine the onions, garlic, salt, caraway seeds and bouillon. Simmer for 5 minutes. Add the rolled shoulder of veal. Add the sauerkraut and paprika. Cover and simmer for about 2 hours, or until tender. Slice and serve hot.
Serves 6. (193 calories per serving.)

BEEF STEW WITH CHEESE DUMPLINGS

3 cans (8 oz. each) Mott's Figure Control Beef Stew
2 egg whites
3 tablespoons grated Swiss or Parmesan cheese

Heat beef stew to bubbling in a one-quart casserole in a 400-degree oven (about fifteen minutes). Meanwhile, beat egg whites stiff, fold in grated cheese, Drop meringue-dumpling mixture by teaspoons on boiling stew and bake about 5 minutes longer, until dumplings are puffed and golden brown.
Serves 4. (145 calories per serving.)

HUNGARIAN SKILLET STEW

2 pounds boneless round steak
Adolph's Seasoned Instant
Meat Tenderizer
1 tablespoon butter or
margarine
1 large onion, sliced thin
1 (No. 2½) can tomatoes

1½ teaspoons paprika
1 teaspoon salt
½ teaspoon pepper
¼ teaspoon Adolph's Granulated Sugar Substitute
1 cup water

Prepare all surfaces of the meat, one side at a time, follow-ing directions on jar of Adolph's Seasoned Instant Meat Tender-izer. Cut meat in 1½-inch cubes.

In hot butter in skillet over low heat, saute onion slices until lightly browned. Stir carefully to avoid sticking. Add cubes of meat a few at a time, browning and stirring with a wooden spoon. Add tomatoes, paprika, salt, pepper and Adolph's Granulated Sugar Substitute. Stir in ⅓ cup of the water. Cover, simmer until meat is tender, about 1¼ hours. Add more water as needed. For thicker consistency, remove cover and let mixture simmer to desired thickness.

Serves 6. (238 calories per serving.)

MEATBALLS IN TOMATO-CRANBERRY SAUCE

2 pounds lean ground beef
½ teaspoon salt
¼ teaspoon pepper
2 slices white bread
2 (8 ounce) cans tomato sauce

1 cup Ocean Spray Dietetic
Cranberry Sauce (see Chapter
8)
Juice of 1 lemon

Soak white bread in water. Blend into ground beef. Add salt and pepper. Form small meatballs. In a medium sized sauce-pan, blend the 2 cans of tomato sauce with the cranberry sauce. Add lemon juice. Add the meatballs and simmer for 1 hour.

Serves 8. (299 calories per serving.)

QUICK LASAGNE

3 cans (8 oz. each) Mott's Figure Control Spaghetti with Meatballs
¾ cup sieved skim milk cottage cheese
¾ teaspoon salt
¾ teaspoon instant minced onion

Pour 1½ cans spaghetti with meatballs into a shallow, rectangular one-quart casserole. Mix cottage cheese with salt and minced onion. Spread on spaghetti. Top with remaining spaghetti. Bake at 350 degrees about thirty minutes, until bubbling hot.

Serves 4. 158 calories each. (Would be 298 calories with regular canned spaghetti and meatballs. Regular lasagne has about 550 calories per serving!)

SAUERBRATEN

4 pounds beef round roast
1 sliced onion
2 bay leaves
1 teaspoon salt
½ teaspoon pepper
½ teaspoon ginger
½ cup vinegar
½ cup water
¼ cup raisins
½ tablespoon Sucaryl solution

Sprinkle meat with salt and pepper. Place in a deep bowl. Add onion slices, bay leaves, vinegar mixed with water, ginger, and Sucaryl. Marinate in the refrigerator overnight, turning occasionally.

Lift meat and onions and a little marinade and place in bottom of Dutch oven. Brown in a 400-degree oven, then cover and reduce heat to 300 degrees, for about 3 hours or until tender. Add more marinade as necessary. Add raisins the last hour of cooking. When ready to serve, strain gravy and thicken with flour. Serve over sliced meat.

283 calories per 4 ounce slice.

APPLE-RAISIN SAUCE

¾ cup seedless raisins
1¼ cups unsweetened apple juice
2 teaspoons Adolph's Granulated Sugar Substitute
2 teaspoons cornstarch

1½ tablespoons butter
¼ teaspoon salt
¼ teaspoon ground ginger
⅛ teaspoon ground cloves
⅛ teaspoon ground allspice

Simmer raisins in apple juice until plump. Combine remaining ingredients; mix thoroughly and add to juice. Continue simmering for about 5 minutes, stirring constantly. Serve piping hot.

Makes about 1 cup of sauce. About 40 calories per tablespoon.

Serve this versatile sauce with baked or broiled ham, pork chops or pork roast, venison, game birds, and/or "planned-over" dishes you want to glamorize.

BARBECUE SAUCE

¼ cup chopped onion
1 cup catsup
½ cup water
¼ cup lemon juice
3 tablespoons Worcestershire
sauce

2 tablespoons vinegar
1½ teaspoons prepared mustard
1 teaspoon Sucaryl solution
½ teaspoon salt
Dash of pepper and cayenne

Combine all ingredients in a small saucepan. Simmer for 20 minutes. Use to baste hamburgers or steaks during broiling. Makes 2 cups. 10 calories per tablespoon.

ORANGE SAUCE

¼ cup lemon juice
1 cup orange juice
2 teaspoons Sucaryl solution
1 tablespoon grated orange peel

½ teaspoon caraway seed
¼ teaspoon marjoram
¼ teaspoon rosemary
1 tablespoon cornstarch

Combine juices and Sucaryl. Set aside. Combine remaining ingredients in a small saucepan. Add a small amount of the juice to make a smooth paste; then add rest of juice. Cook over low heat, stirring constantly, until slightly thick. Spoon sauce over sliced cooked chicken and heat in a 350-degree oven for 15 minutes.

Makes 1¼ cups sauce. 28 calories each ¼ cup.

Chapter Seven

VITAL VEGETABLES

Not only do you have to know your onions, you have to know your peas and cucumbers too!

By studying the calorie chart in the back of the book, you will discover that vegetables vary greatly in their calorie content. Lima beans and peas are just bursting with calories, while asparagus, green beans, tomatoes and broccoli are co-operatively low and tasty.

Concentrate on these lower-calorie vegetables and season them with other low-calorie products. Or use low-calorie products as the seasoning agent for fresh vegetables from your local market.

Either way, vegetables add color and bulk to your meals, besides providing an excellent source of vitamins and minerals for your good health. By following the recipes in this section, you will be able to serve surprise vegetable dishes that will satisfy a hearty appetite. They have been streamlined to meet the most weight-conscious specifications!

ACORN SQUASH

1 acorn squash
A few dashes of Adolph's Granulated Sugar Substitute
1 (8 ounce) can S & W Nutradiet Sweet Peas

Slice acorn squash crosswise into 1-inch rings. Remove seeds. Cook squash in a small amount of salted boiling water, in a covered skillet, until tender. Drain, sprinkle each ring with a dash of granulated sugar substitute. Serve with a tablespoon of peas in the center.

Serves 8. (27 calories per serving with peas.)

ACORN SQUASH WITH APPLE SAUCE

2 acorn squash
½ (8 ounce) can S & W Nutradiet Apple Sauce
½ teaspoon salt
¼ teaspoon nutmeg

Cut acorn squash in half, lengthwise. Remove seeds and sprinkle with salt. Bake in a 400-degree oven for 30 minutes, cut side down in a shallow pan. Remove squash from shells, reserving shells for stuffing. Mash squash with ½ can apple sauce. Add nutmeg. Salt to taste. Pile mixture back into shells. Bake for an additional 20 minutes until browned.

Serves 4. (43 calories per serving.)

ASPARAGUS AU GRATIN

1 (8 ounce) can S & W Nutradiet Asparagus
1 tablespoon fine breadcrumbs
1 tablespoon grated parmesan cheese

Arrange asparagus spears in a small shallow casserole. Blend the breadcrumbs and grated cheese together and sprinkle evenly over the asparagus. Broil for a few minutes, until the cheese melts. Serve hot.

Serves 2. (42 calories per serving.)

ASPARAGUS RING

3 10-ounce packages frozen asparagus, cooked
1 teaspoon salt
¼ teaspoon pepper

2 eggs
Breadcrumbs
1 can Mott's Figure Control White Sauce

Separate eggs. Beat yolks. Add salt and pepper. Chop asparagus and add to yolk mixture. Blend in white sauce.

Beat egg whites stiff and gently fold into mixture. Lightly butter a 6-cup ring mold and dust with breadcrumbs. Pour in asparagus mixture and set ring mold in a pan of water to bake for 40 minutes in a 350-degree oven. Unmold to serve. Can fill center with tiny whole cooked carrots.

Serves 10. (47 calories per serving.)

GREEN BEANS PARMESAN

1 (8 ounce) can S & W Nutradiet Cut Green Beans
1 teaspoon grated parmesan cheese
Salt to taste

Drain hot green beans. Sprinkle with parmesan cheese and salt to taste. Cover to let cheese melt. Serve hot.

Serves 2. (21 calories per serving.)

SAVORY GREEN BEANS

2½ cups cooked or canned whole green beans
¼ cup thin onion slices
¼ cup liquid from cooking beans, or from can
½ cup Mott's Figure Control Italian Dressing

Heat beans and onion slices in vegetable liquid. Add Italian dressing, toss all together, and serve hot.

Serves 4. 34 calories per serving. (Would be 145 calories a serving with regular dressing!)

ZESTY GREEN BEANS

> 1 (8 ounce) can S & W Nutradiet Green Beans
> ¼ cup cocktail onions
> 1 tablespoon sweet pickle relish
> 3 tablespoons Mott's Figure Control Italian Dressing

Add cocktail onions to the green beans. Heat and drain. Blend the sweet pickle relish into the Italian dressing and pour the mixture over the beans just before serving.

Serves 2. (46 calories per serving.)

HARVARD BEETS

> 1 (1 pound) can sliced beets
> 1½ to 2 teaspoons Adolph's Granulated Sugar Substitute
> 3 teaspoons cornstarch
>   Dash of salt
> ¼ cup vinegar

Drain beets, reserving liquid. In saucepan blend Adolph's Granulated Sugar Substitute, cornstarch and salt. Stir in vinegar and reserved beet juice. Cook, stirring constantly, until smooth and thickened. Add beets and heat.

Serves 4. (39 calories per serving.)

ORANGE GLAZED BEETS

> 2 tablespoons butter
> 2 teaspoons cornstarch
> ¼ teaspoon salt
> 1 tablespoon Sucaryl solution
> 1 teaspoon cider vinegar
>
> 2 teaspoons grated orange rind
> ½ cup orange juice
> 3 cups cooked sliced beets
>   (1½ pounds)

Melt butter in saucepan. Blend in cornstarch and salt. Add
Sucaryl, vinegar, orange rind and juice. Cook over medium
heat until smooth and thick, stirring constantly. Add beets and
simmer over low heat about 10 minutes until heated through.
Serves 6. 79 calories per serving.

PICKLED BEETS

    1 (1 pound) can regular sliced beets, drained
    1 medium onion, sliced paper thin
    1 cup cider vinegar
    1 teaspoon Adolph's Granulated Sugar Substitute

Blend beet juice, vinegar, and sugar substitute. Pour over
beets and onions, and marinate in the refrigerator for several
hours. Serve cold.
Serves 4. (47 calories per serving.)

SAVORY BEETS

Substitute canned sliced beets for the green beans in Savory
Green Beans recipe. Use beet juice as liquid.
Serves 6. 41 calories per serving. (Would be 115 calories
each with regular dressing.)

BROCCOLI AU GRATIN

    1 package frozen broccoli, cooked
    ½ can Mott's Figure Control White Sauce
    1 tablespoon finely grated breadcrumbs
    1 tablespoon grated parmesan cheese
    A dash of paprika

Arrange cooked broccoli in bottom of a shallow casserole.
Cover with white sauce. Sprinkle evenly with grated breadcrumbs and grated parmesan cheese. Sprinkle with a dash of

paprika. Bake in a moderate oven (350 degrees) for fifteen minutes. Serve hot.

Serves 4. (53 calories per serving.)

BROCCOLI WITH CHEESE SAUCE

1 package frozen broccoli, cooked
4 ounces Mott's Figure Control Welsh Rarebit
1 tablespoon diced pimento

Place cooked broccoli in a shallow casserole. Spread the Welsh rarebit over the top. Bake for 10 minutes, or until heated through, in a 350-degree oven. Garnish with diced pimento.

Serves 4. (33 calories per serving.)

CABBAGE AU GRATIN

1 large cabbage, cooked
1 can Mott's Figure Control White Sauce
¼ cup grated parmesan cheese

½ teaspoon salt
¼ teaspoon pepper
¼ cup cracker crumbs

Slice cooked cabbage thin, and arrange one layer in a baking dish. Blend cheese, salt and pepper into the white sauce. Spread half the sauce over the sliced cabbage, and cover with another layer of cabbage. Top with remaining sauce. Sprinkle with cracker crumbs and bake in a 350-degree oven until crumbs are browned.

Serves 8. (70 calories per serving.)

SWEET-SOUR GERMAN CABBAGE

2 tablespoons butter
6 cups raw, shredded red cabbage, washed and drained
1 medium onion, sliced in rings

¼ cup water
½ cup vinegar
1 teaspoon Sucaryl solution

Melt butter in a large saucepan. Add cabbage (use only water which still clings to leaves). Cook covered over low heat until tender, stirring occasionally to prevent sticking. Add onion rings, water, vinegar and Sucaryl. Cover and cook about 10 minutes longer.

Serves 6. (68 calories per serving.)

SWEET-AND-SOUR RED CABBAGE

1 medium head red cabbage, shredded
1 large apple, diced
2 cups hot water
⅔ cup vinegar
¾ teaspoon Adolph's Granulated Sugar Substitute
½ teaspoon salt

In a medium skillet, heat all ingredients except cabbage and apple. When hot, add cabbage and apple and cook over low flame until tender.

Serves 6. (29 calories per serving.)

MINTED CARROTS

1 (8 ounce) can S & W Nutradiet Sliced Carrots
1 teaspoon crushed mint leaves

Heat carrots and mint leaves together in a small saucepan. Drain and serve hot.

Serves 2. (24 calories per serving.)

CAULIFLOWER NEWBURG

1 medium head fresh cauliflower, cooked
½ can Mott's Figure Control Newburg Sauce
Dash of paprika

Arrange drained, cooked, hot cauliflower head on a shallow serving dish. Pour hot Newburg sauce over the top of the cauliflower. Sprinkle with a dash of paprika.

Serves 6. (32 calories per serving.)

CAULIFLOWER AU GRATIN

1 medium head of cauliflower, cooked
1 (8 ounce) can Claybourne Dietetic Cream of Mushroom Soup
1 tablespoon sherry
1 tablespoon grated parmesan cheese
   Dash of paprika

In a small saucepan, blend and heat the mushroom soup, sherry, and parmesan cheese. Arrange the drained cooked cauliflower in a shallow serving dish. Pour hot sauce over the cauliflower. Sprinkle with paprika.

Serves 6. (32 calories per serving.)

PICKLED CUCUMBERS

2 cucumbers, peeled and sliced thin
1 medium onion, sliced thin
1 cup vinegar
½ teaspoon salt
¼ teaspoon pepper
½ teaspoon Adolph's Granulated Sugar Substitute

Blend vinegar, salt, pepper, and the sugar substitute in a small deep bowl. Marinate the cucumber slices and onion slices together for several hours. Serve cold.

Serves 6. (14 calories per serving.)

MUSHROOM CASSEROLE

1 pound fresh mushrooms, whole
1 (8 ounce) can Claybourne Dietetic Cream of Mushroom Soup
½ cup prepared stuffing mix
1 onion, sliced thin
½ cup skim milk

In a small casserole, blend the condensed mushroom soup with the milk. Add the whole mushroom caps, sliced stems, sliced onion and most of the prepared stuffing. Mix through, then scatter the rest of the prepared stuffing over the top. Bake in a 350-degree oven for 30 minutes.

Serves 6. (68 calories per serving.)

PEAS WITH MUSHROOMS

1 (8 ounce) can S & W Nutradiet Sweet Peas
1 cup sliced mushrooms
2 tablespoons diced pimento

Drain the juice from the can of peas into a small skillet. Add sliced fresh mushrooms and simmer for 10 minutes. Add peas and diced pimento. Heat and serve.

Serves 4. (32 calories per serving.)

STUFFED BAKED WHITE POTATOES

4 scrubbed white baking potatoes
¼ cup cottage cheese
2 tablespoons chopped fresh chives

Bake potatoes until soft and mealy. Cut lengthwise one-third of the way down, discarding the tops and reserving the two-third "boats" for refilling. Scoop out the potato meat. Mash with cottage cheese and fresh chives. Pile lightly back into the "boats" swirling the exposed mound on top. Garnish with a dash of paprika on each. Bake for an additional 15 minutes at 350 degrees. Serve immediately.

Serves 4. (102 calories per serving.)

CREAMED SPINACH

1 package frozen chopped spinach, cooked
1 teaspoon dried grated onion
4 ounces Mott's Figure Control White Sauce
   A few dashes of nutmeg
½ teaspoon salt

Cook chopped spinach in a small amount of water containing the dried grated onion. Drain. Blend white sauce through. Add a few dashes of nutmeg and the salt. Serve hot. Serves 3. (43 calories per serving.)

BROILED TOMATOES WITH CHIVES

4 medium tomatoes
1 tablespoon chopped chives
1 tablespoon Loeb Gluten Breadcrumbs
   Salt to taste

Cut tomatoes in half. Sprinkle with salt, breadcrumbs and chopped chives. Broil for 15 minutes. Serve hot.

Two pieces per serving, serves 4. 33 calories per serving.

ZUCCHINI PARMESAN

4 cups sliced zucchini
1 small sliced onion
2 tablespoons water
1 teaspoon salt
¼ teaspoon pepper
1 tablespoon butter or margarine
3 tablespoons parmesan cheese

Combine all ingredients except the parmesan cheese in a skillet. Cover and cook for 1 minute, then remove cover and cook for another 4 minutes, turning the mixture as it cooks. Sprinkle with cheese. Serve hot.

Serves 8. (44 calories per serving.)

Chapter Eight

SYLPHLIKE SALADS

With all the low-calorie dressings available, one could merely rotate them on lettuce every day and have tasty salads. But that would eliminate the exploration of endless variations of low-calorie recipes that serve as side accompaniments to dinner or in larger quantities as luncheon dishes.

Fresh, clean, crisp vegetables are a vital necessity when planning a tossed salad. Wash, drain, then wrap your greens in paper toweling and place in the crisping bin of your refrigerator. Apply your dressings just minutes before serving and you will avoid wilted, tired looking salads.

By using gelatin substitutes in molded salads, you save hundreds of calories per mold and still maintain high standards of tasty flavors and textures. You will find many gelatin molds in this chapter that you can serve with confidence to anyone. You will also find exotic combinations of fruits and vegetables designed to lift your morale as you lower your girth.

Your guests will not tag them as dietetic until you burst forth with the good news!

CELERY SEED DRESSING

2 teaspoons cornstarch
¾ cup water
½ teaspoon Adolph's Granulated Sugar Substitute
½ teaspoon dry mustard
¼ teaspoon salt
¼ teaspoon onion salt
¼ teaspoon paprika
1 tablespoon celery seed
¼ cup lemon or lime juice
1 tablespoon salad oil

Using a small saucepan, add water slowly to cornstarch and blend until smooth; add Adolph's Granulated Sugar Substitute; cook over low flame until mixture is clear and thickened; remove from heat and cool.

Blend spices and celery seed together; add to cornstarch mixture. Beat in lemon juice and oil. Store in refrigerator. Shake well before serving.

Makes about one cup. 4 calories per teaspoon.

CHICKEN SALAD RING MOLD

4 1-ounce envelopes Lemon D-Zerta Gelatin
3½ cups hot chicken broth (can be made with bouillon cubes)
1 teaspoon salt
1 teaspoon finely minced onion
4 tablespoons lemon juice
1½ cups cubed fresh tomatoes
½ cup dietetic mayonnaise
2 cups diced cooked chicken
1 cup finely diced celery
2 tablespoons finely minced dill pickle

Dissolve the gelatin in the hot chicken broth, add salt and lemon juice. Add minced onion, and chill until slightly thickened.

Mix remaining ingredients together, and add to chilled gelatin mixture. Blend thoroughly and fill a two-quart mold with the mixture. Chill until firm. Unmold on crisp salad greens.

Serves 8. (135 calories per serving.)

CUCUMBER SALAD

1 sliced cucumber
2 tomatoes, diced
½ red onion, peeled and sliced
1 small head lettuce

3 tablespoons Mott's Figure
Control French Dressing
½ clove garlic

Rub bowl with garlic. Tear lettuce into bite sized pieces. Arrange sliced cucumber in a circle around the edge of the bowl. Fill center with diced tomatoes. Scatter sliced red onion rings over the top. Just before serving, add the French dressing. Serves 6. (23 calories per serving.)

DIETETIC CRANBERRY SAUCE

4 cups (1 pound) Ocean Spray Fresh Cranberries
1½ cups water
4 teaspoons Sucaryl

Combine cranberries, water and Sucaryl in a saucepan. Bring to a boil, then lower heat and simmer until berries pop open (about 10 minutes). Chill to serve.

Makes 1 to 1½ pints. 28 calories per 4-ounce serving.

CRANBERRY-ORANGE GELATIN

2 cups Ocean Spray Cranberries
1 orange
2 tablespoons Sucaryl solution
3 envelopes orange D-Zerta Gelatin
2 cups hot water

Put cranberries and orange, including rind, through food grinder (coarse blade). Stir in sweetener. Chill. Dissolve D-Zerta in hot water. Refrigerate until mixture begins to thicken. Add cranberry orange mixture. Pour into a greased mold or individual molds.

Serves 6. (41 calories per serving.)

CRANBERRY-ORANGE RELISH

4 cups (1 pound) Ocean Spray Fresh Cranberries
2 oranges, quartered and seeded
4 tablespoons Sucaryl solution

Put cranberries and oranges, including rind, through food grinder (coarse blade). Stir in sweetener. Chill at least 3 hours before serving. Makes about 2 cups.

Serves 8. (47 calories per serving.)

TANGY SALAD

1 head lettuce, small
½ cup thinly sliced scallions
5 or 6 thinly sliced radishes
3 tablespoons Mott's Figure Control Italian-Style Dressing

Tear lettuce into bite sized pieces. Add sliced scallions and sliced radishes. Just before serving, add Italian dressing.

Serves 6. (14 calories per serving.)

CRISPY SALAD BOWL

1 small head lettuce
2 cups chopped raw spinach
8 sliced radishes
3 tomatoes
½ head raw cauliflower
1 sliced onion
1 clove garlic
Mott's Figure Control Italian Dressing

Rub the salad bowl lightly with garlic. Wash and drain all vegetables. Tear lettuce into bite sized pieces. Place in salad bowl. Mound center with spinach and surround with wedges of tomatoes, small flowerets of cauliflower, and sliced radishes. Top with thinly sliced onion rings. Serve with low-calorie Italian-style dressing.

Serves 8. (36 calories per serving, without dressing.)

WESTERN SALAD BOWL

1 small head lettuce
2 tomatoes, cut in wedges
2 stalks celery, cut in 1-inch lengths
6 sliced radishes

4 scallions, chopped
½ green pepper, sliced thin
¼ cup Diamel Blue Cheese Dietetic Dressing

Tear lettuce into bite sized pieces. Arrange other vegetables attractively on top. Pour dressing and toss, just before serving.

Serves 6. (23 calories per serving.)

LEMON-FLAVORED RICE MOLD

½ cup rice
½ teaspoon salt
½ cup boiling water
2½ cups skim milk
1 tablespoon unflavored gelatin
¼ cup cold water

4 eggs, separated
2 tablespoons Sucaryl solution
1 tablespoon lemon rind
2 tablespoons lemon juice
1 teaspoon vanilla

In the top of a double boiler, combine rice, salt, and boiling water; bring to a boil and cook about 2 minutes. Add milk and cook over hot water until rice is tender (about 10 minutes). Soften gelatin in cold water. Combine egg yolks, Sucaryl, lemon rind, lemon juice, and vanilla. Slowly add some of the hot rice mixture to the egg yolk mixture; return to double boiler and cook 5 minutes longer, stirring occasionally. Remove from heat, stir in softened gelatin until dissolved, chill slightly. Beat egg whites until stiff peaks form; fold into rice mixture. Spoon into an 8-cup mold and chill until set. To serve, unmold and garnish with orange slices and green grapes.

Serves 8. (114 calories per serving.)

HOT POTATO SALAD

    4 medium boiled potatoes
    ¼ cup Mott's Figure Control Italian Dressing
    2 tablespoons finely minced fresh onion
    6 tablespoons Mott's Figure Control Whipped Dressing
  1½ teaspoons chopped fresh chives or parsley

Peel hot potatoes, cut in chunks. Mix with Italian dressing and minced onion, let stand a few minutes to absorb. Coat with whipped dressing. Sprinkle with chopped chives or parsley and serve hot.

Serves 6. About 80 calories per serving (compared with 208 calories per serving if prepared with regular dressing).

SALAD ITALIENNE

    1 cup cooked whole green beans
    ¼ cup Mott's Figure Control Italian Dressing
    1 (2 ounce) can mushrooms, drained
    1 medium pimento, cut in strips

Marinate beans in Italian dressing. Chill. At serving time, heap mushrooms in the center of a platter. Surround with marinated beans. Garnish with pimento.

Serves 4. 20 calories per serving (with regular Italian dressing this would be 55 calories per serving).

RASPBERRY APRICOT DELIGHT

    1 envelope raspberry D-Zerta
    Dash of salt
    Dash of cinnamon
    1 cup hot water
    4 halves drained canned unsweetened apricots

Combine D-Zerta, salt, and cinnamon. Add hot water and stir until D-Zerta is dissolved. Chill until slightly thickened. Place two apricot halves in each glass serving dish. Pour D-Zerta mixture over apricots. Chill until firm.

Serves 2. (18 calories per serving.)

SPICED PEAR MOLD

    1 envelope cherry D-Zerta
    Dash of salt
    Dash of ginger
    Dash of cinnamon
    1 cup hot water
    ⅓ cup diced drained unsweetened pears

Combine 1 envelope cherry D-Zerta, a dash of salt, dash of ginger, and dash of cinnamon. Add 1 cup hot water; stir until D-Zerta is dissolved. Chill until slightly thickened. Then fold in pears. Pour into molds. Chill until firm. Serve with cottage cheese on crisp salad greens.

Serves 2. (27 calories per serving.)

SHAMROCK PEARS

    2 packages lime flavored D-Zerta
    1 cup hot water
    1 cup low-calorie ginger ale
    1 can drained dietetic pack pear halves

Dissolve the lime gelatin in the hot water. Add ginger ale, mixing thoroughly. Arrange pears in a small flat pan, cut side up. Pour in gelatin. Chill until firm. Cut into squares containing each pear half.

Serves 4. (31 calories per serving.)

LIME COTTAGE CHEESE SALAD

2 envelopes lime D-Zerta
⅛ teaspoon salt
2 teaspoons vinegar
2 cups hot water

½ cup cottage cheese
2 teaspoons pimento
1 teaspoon grated onion

Dissolve D-Zerta as directed. Add salt and vinegar. Pour 1 cup of mixture into molds. Chill until almost firm. Chill remaining D-Zerta until slightly thickened. Fold in cottage cheese, pimento, and grated onion. Pour over layer in molds. Chill. Serve unmolded on crisp salad greens.

Serves 4. (38 calories per serving.)

SPRING SALAD

1 envelope lime D-Zerta
½ teaspoon salt
1 cup hot water
1½ teaspoons vinegar

⅓ cup finely diced cucumber
¼ cup finely diced celery
2 tablespoons finely cut green onions

Dissolve D-Zerta and salt in hot water. Add vinegar. Chill until slightly thickened. Add remaining ingredients. Pour into molds. Chill until firm. Unmold.

Serves 2. (18 calories per serving.)

CONFETTI SALAD

1 envelope lemon D-Zerta
1 cup hot water
Dash of salt
¼ teaspoon minced onion

2 teaspoons diced pimento
¼ cup very small pieces raw cauliflower

Dissolve 1 envelope of lemon D-Zerta in 1 cup hot water. Add a dash of salt and the minced onion. Chill until slightly thickened. Then fold in diced pimento and raw cauliflower. Pour mixture into molds. Chill until firm. Unmold on crisp salad greens. Serve with a low-calorie salad dressing, if desired.

Serves 2. (15 calories per serving, without dressing.)

WALDORF SALAD

    2 Delicious apples
    ½ cup Mott's Figure Control Whipped Dressing
    ¼ cup seedless raisins
    4 celery stalks
    ¼ cup broken walnuts

Core apples, dice without peeling. Mix 6 tablespoons whipped dressing with apples to prevent browning. Toss raisins in remaining dressing. Thinly slice celery, diagonally. On one side of salad bowl, heap apple mixture; on other side, heap celery; pile raisins between. Toss all together just before serving.

Serves 6. 108 calories per serving. (If prepared with mayonnaise, calories per serving would be 223.)

LUNCHEON SALAD

    1 envelope lemon D-Zerta
    ½ teaspoon salt
    1 cup hot water
    1 teaspoon vinegar
    ½ cup flaked tuna fish or crab meat or diced shrimps or chicken
    1 tablespoon chopped celery
    1 tablespoon chopped green pepper
    1 teaspoon chopped onion

Dissolve D-Zerta and salt in hot water. Add vinegar. Chill until slightly thickened. Fold in remaining ingredients. Pour into molds. Chill until firm. Unmold and serve on lettuce leaf.

Serves 2. 70 calories per serving with tuna. 67 calories per serving with chicken. 48 calories per serving with shrimps or crab meat.

PINEAPPLE SHRIMP SALAD MOLD

2 envelopes lime D-Zerta Gelatin
1 cup hot water
2½ cups dietetic crushed pineapple
2 medium cucumbers, peeled and chopped
4 tablespoons lemon juice
½ teaspoon Adolph's Granulated Sugar Substitute
¼ teaspoon salt
1 pound shrimps, cleaned and cooked
½ cup low-calorie dietetic Italian dressing

Dissolve gelatin in the cup of hot water. Drain crushed pineapple. Add enough cold water to the syrup to measure ¾ cup. Blend into gelatin mixture.

Add lemon juice, sugar substitute and salt. Chill slightly. Add chopped cucumbers and crushed pineapple. Pour into oiled 1-quart ring mold. Chill until firm. Unmold on crisp salad greens before serving.

Marinate 1 pound shrimps, cleaned and cooked, in the Italian dressing. Fill center of the mold with the shrimps. Garnish with strips of pimento.

Serves 6. 64 calories per serving without shrimps. 101 calories per serving with shrimps.

TOMATO ASPIC

1 tablespoon unflavored gelatin
2 cups Mott's Figure Control Tomato Juice
1 teaspoon grated onion
1 teaspoon salt

Soften the unflavored gelatin in ¼ cup of cold tomato juice. Boil the remaining tomato juice. Add onion and salt; then add

softened gelatin, stirring until the gelatin is dissolved. Pour
into 1 large mold or into individual molds. Chill until firm. Unmold and serve on crisp fresh greens.

Serves 4. (27 calories per serving.)

TUNA STUFFED TOMATO

3 medium firm tomatoes
1 can Chicken of the Sea Dietetic Tuna
1 small apple, diced
2 stalks celery, diced
2 tablespoons Loeb's Dietetic Mayonnaise

Place each tomato on a lettuce cup. Core, and slice into
quarters part way to the bottom.

In a small bowl, mash tuna; add diced apple and diced
celery. Mix through with dietetic mayonnaise. Put one-third of
the mixture into the center of each tomato. Garnish with cold
canned asparagus.

Serves 3. (134 calories per serving without garnish.)

CHERRY-SHERRY VALENTINE

1 tablespoon unflavored gelatin
¼ cup sherry
1 1-pound can sour red cherries,
water-packed
1 tablespoon lemon juice
1 tablespoon Sucaryl solution
½ cup non-fat dry milk
½ cup iced water

Soften gelatin in sherry; dissolve over hot water. Add drained
cherries, lemon juice and Sucaryl. Chill until mixture begins
to thicken. Combine dry milk and iced water; beat on high
speed of mixer until of consistency of whipped cream. Fold into
gelatin mixture. Spoon into a 7-cup heart mold. Chill until firm.

Serves 8. (69 calories per serving.)

RASPBERRY SALAD RING

3 cups fresh red raspberries
1½ tablespoons Sucaryl solution
2 tablespoons gelatin
½ cup lemon juice
2 cups boiling water

Crush 1 cup of the raspberries; force through a sieve to remove seeds; add Sucaryl. Soften gelatin in lemon juice; dissolve in boiling water. Stir in sieved raspberries. Chill until mixture begins to thicken. Fold in remaining raspberries; chill until set. Unmold on salad greens, and fill center as desired with cottage cheese or chicken salad.

Serves 8. (38 calories per serving.)

GRAPEFRUIT ASPIC

2 tablespoons unflavored gelatin
½ cup water
3 cups unsweetened grapefruit juice
3 tablespoons Sucaryl solution
3 tablespoons sherry
2 cups fresh grapefruit sections
¾ cup finely chopped celery

Soften gelatin in cold water. Heat grapefruit juice to boiling; add to gelatin, stirring to dissolve. Add Sucaryl and sherry. Arrange a few of the grapefruit sections in the bottom of a lightly oiled 5-cup ring mold to form a decorative pattern; add enough of the gelatin to cover; chill until set. Chill remaining gelatin until it begins to thicken; fold in remaining grapefruit sections and celery. Spoon mixture into mold and chill until firm. To serve, unmold and, if desired, fill center of ring with cottage cheese. Garnish with watercress or other greens.

Serves 10. 57 calories per serving, without cottage cheese.

JELLIED AMBROSIA

3 tablespoons unflavored gelatin
¼ cup cold water
4 cups fresh orange juice
1 tablespoon lemon juice

4½ teaspoons Sucaryl solution
1 cup orange sections
1 cup banana slices
⅓ cup flaked coconut

Soften gelatin in cold water; dissolve over boiling water. Stir in orange juice, lemon juice and Sucaryl. Chill until mixture begins to thicken. Fold in fruit and coconut. Spoon into a lightly oiled 5-cup mold. Chill until set. To serve, unmold and garnish, if desired, with additional coconut and banana slices.

Serves 8. (109 calories per serving.)

AMBER APPLE JELLY SALAD

2 tablespoons unflavored gelatin
½ cup cold water
1 quart apple juice
1 tablespoon Sucaryl solution

¾ cup diced unpeeled apple
¾ cup grape halves
1 8½-ounce can Libby dietetic pineapple tidbits, drained

Soften gelatin in cold water. Heat 2 cups of the apple juice; add to gelatin, stirring to dissolve. Add remaining apple juice and Sucaryl. Chill until mixture begins to thicken. Add diced apple, grapes, and pineapple. Spoon into a lightly oiled 6-cup mold; chill until set. Unmold and serve on salad greens.

Serves 12. (70 calories per serving.)

CHERRY VALENTINE SALAD

2 tablespoons unflavored gelatin
⅓ cup cold water
1 1-pound can water-pack sour cherries
1 tablespoon Sucaryl solution

½ cup unsweetened apple sauce
½ cup finely chopped celery
¼ cup non-fat dry milk
¼ cup ice water

Soften gelatin in cold water; dissolve over boiling water. Force cherries and liquid through food mill. Add dissolved gelatin, stirring well to blend. Add Sucaryl and apple sauce; chill until mixture begins to thicken. Add celery. Combine dry milk and ice water in small bowl of mixer; beat on high speed until of consistency of heavy cream; fold into gelatin mixture. Spoon into a lightly oiled 1-quart heart-shaped mold, or into 12 individual molds. Chill until set. Unmold and serve on crisp salad greens.

Serves 12. (37 calories per serving.)

CRANBERRY BUFFET SALAD

2 tablespoons unflavored gelatin
½ cup cold water
2 cups Ocean Spray Fresh Cranberries
1 cup water
3 tablespoons Sucaryl solution
2 cups Sucaryl sweetened non-
 caloric ginger ale
1½ cups diced apples
1½ cups diced celery

Soften gelatin in the ½ cup cold water. Combine cran-berries and 1 cup water; cook until skins pop. Force through a sieve; add Sucaryl. Add sieved cranberries to gelatin, stirring to dissolve. Cool slightly. Stir in ginger ale. Refrigerate until mixture begins to thicken. Fold in apples and celery. Pour into a 1-quart mold; chill until set. Unmold and serve on crisp salad greens.

Serves 8. (40 calories per serving.)

ORANGE MINT JELLY

3 tablespoons unflavored gelatin
¾ cup cold water
⅓ cup minced mint leaves
1½ cups boiling water
2 tablespoons Sucaryl solution
1½ cups orange juice
½ cup lemon juice

Soften gelatin in cold water. Steep mint leaves in boiling water for several minutes; strain, saving the liquid. Add softened gelatin, stirring to dissolve. Add remaining ingredients; pour into a 4-cup mold; chill until set. Serve with roast lamb, chicken, baked ham, as the salad accompaniment.

Serves 6. (49 calories per serving.)

WHITE-CAPPED STRAWBERRY-PINEAPPLE SALAD

First Layer

1 tablespoon unflavored gelatin	Dash of salt
½ cup cold water	2 tablespoons lemon juice
1 cup boiling water	⅓ cup buttermilk
1 tablespoon Sucaryl solution	⅓ cup non-fat dry milk

Second Layer

1 tablespoon unflavored gelatin	2 teaspoons Sucaryl solution
1½ cups unsweetened pineapple juice	1 cup fresh strawberries, sliced
1 tablespoon lemon juice	1 5-ounce jar Mott's Figure Control Pineapple Topping

First Layer: Soften gelatin in cold water; dissolve in boiling water. Add Sucaryl, salt and lemon juice, blending well. Combine buttermilk and dry milk; beat on high speed of mixer. until thick and fluffy. Blend into gelatin mixture. Spoon into the bottom of a 6-cup mold; chill until set.

Second Layer: Soften gelatin in ½ cup of the pineapple juice; dissolve over boiling water; add remaining 1 cup pineapple juice, lemon juice and Sucaryl. Chill until mixture begins to set; fold in strawberries and pineapple topping. Carefully pour over first layer; chill until set. To serve, unmold on salad greens.

Serves 6. (94 calories per serving.)

Chapter Nine

EXTRAVAGANT EGGS

You'll cackle with pleasure when you discover the wonderful world of eggs. Their delicate shells are packed with protein and only average 75 calories each, when boiled. Surely here is a streamlining food that is not be overlooked by the serious dieter.

Eggs may be served at any meal in a variety of forms, from simple breakfast styles to fluffy soufflés. The color of the shell varies in acceptance in many parts of the country, but actually there is no profound difference in quality, flavor or effectiveness when cooking with brown or white shelled eggs.

Soufflés, long considered difficult to perfect for even the most adept cook, are simple if a few basic rules are followed. First, always use a straight-sided round casserole or soufflé dish to permit the soufflé to rise to its maximum height. Use the size dish recommended in the recipe. A too large dish will cause the mixture to spread out and be too thin to rise properly. A too small dish will cause the soufflé to rise and spill over the top. Remember that hot soufflés must be served immediately, for they do begin to fall as they cool.

Whites that are kept at room temperature for several hours

before beating will have greater volume. Eggs should always be cooked with a low heat to prevent a tough texture.

Sponge cakes and Angel Food cakes are particularly high in egg ingredients and low in calories, as compared to other cake recipes.

Rich in vitamins, eggs are an excellent choice for everyone, but particularly for those who are avoiding carbohydrates and who seek low-calorie high-protein foods. Many of these egg recipes will make you fall in love at first bite!

OMELETS

2 large eggs
1 tablespoon butter
1 tablespoon milk
¼ teaspoon salt

Melt butter in a small skillet over a low flame. Meanwhile beat eggs, add milk and salt. Pour into skillet. When golden on one side, turn until other side is golden too. Remove from stove and flip onto a plate. Spread one half the surface of the omelet with a filling, and cover with other half. Eat immediately.

Serves 2. (110 calories per person, plus calories for filling.)

FILLINGS:

Add 25 calories for 2 tablespoons uncreamed cottage cheese. Add 14½ calories for 4 tablespoons Louis Sherry dietetic preserves, any flavor.

Add 18 calories for 1 ounce of Mott's Figure Control Welsh Rarebit Cheese Sauce.

BAKED BRANDY SOUFFLE

2 tablespoons butter
2 tablespoons flour
½ cup skim milk
⅛ teaspoon salt

2 tablespoons Grand Marnier or other brandy
5 eggs, separated
1 tablespoon Sucaryl solution

Melt butter in small saucepan. Blend in flour and salt; slowly add milk. Cook over medium heat, stirring constantly, until thickened. Pour into large bowl; add brandy and well beaten egg yolks. Combine egg whites and Sucaryl; beat until stiff peaks form.

Gradually fold egg mixture into beaten egg whites. Pour into a greased 1-quart soufflé dish. Set in a pan of hot water, and bake in a 325-degree oven for 1 hour. Serve immediately. Serves 6. (124 calories per serving.)

APRICOT SOUFFLE

4 eggs
1 teaspoon soft shortening
½ teaspoon Adolph's Granulated Sugar Substitute,
   blended with ½ teaspoon
   cinnamon

1 cup apricot purée
3 tablespoons flour
2 teaspoons Adolph's Granulated Sugar Substitute

To make apricot purée, cook ¼ pound dried apricots in 1½ cups water until tender. Purée, using all liquid.

Separate eggs, putting whites into medium sized bowl and yolks into smaller bowl. Lightly grease a 1-quart soufflé dish or 6-cup baking dish with the shortening. Coat sides and bottom of dish with the cinnamon mixture.

In a large saucepan, combine apricot purée and flour; cook over low heat, stirring constantly, until mixture thickens. Remove from heat; blend in Adolph's Granulated Sugar Substitute.

Beat egg yolks slightly; blend into hot apricot mixture. Cool.

Beat egg whites just stiff enough to hold their shape, but still moist; lightly fold beaten egg whites into apricot mixture until very few streaks of apricot or egg white are left.

Pour into prepared soufflé dish. Bake at 350 degrees for 35-40 minutes, or until top is firm and puffy golden. Serve immediately. Serves 6. (170 calories per serving.)

PRUNE SOUFFLE

Substitute 1 cup prune purée for apricot purée. To make prune purée, cook 1 8-ounce package dried prunes in 1½ cups water until tender. Purée, using all liquid.
Serves 6. (170 calories per serving.)

APPLE SOUFFLE

Substitute 1 cup canned unsweetened dietetic apple sauce (8-ounce can) for apricot purée. Add ¼ teaspoon cinnamon to apple sauce.
Serves 6. (86 calories per serving.)

SQUASH SOUFFLE

4 eggs
1 teaspoon soft shortening
½ teaspoon cinnamon, blended with:
½ teaspoon Adolph's Granulated Sugar Substitute

1 12-ounce package frozen thawed squash
3 tablespoons flour
2 teaspoons Adolph's Granulated Sugar Substitute

Separate eggs, putting whites into medium sized bowl and yolks into smaller bowl. Lightly grease a 1-quart soufflé dish or 6-cup baking dish with the shortening. Coat the sides and bottom of dish with the cinnamon mixture. Combine squash and flour in a large saucepan; cook over low heat, stirring constantly until mixture thickens. Remove from heat; blend in the granulated sugar substitute.
Beat egg yolks slightly; blend into hot squash mixture; cool. Beat egg white just stiff enough to hold their shape, but while

still moist. Lightly fold beaten egg whites into squash mixture until very few streaks of squash or egg whites are left.

Pour into prepared soufflé dish. Bake at 350 degrees for 35-40 minutes, or until top is firm and puffy-golden. Serve immediately. Can add ¼ teaspoon nutmeg or pumpkin pie spice to squash.

Serves 6. (77 calories per serving.)

GLUTEN MACARONI SOUFFLE

½ cup Diamel Gluten Macaroni
1 cup scalded skim milk
⅔ cup breadcrumbs
1 cup grated American cheese
2 egg yolks, beaten

2 egg whites, whipped stiff
3 tablespoons diced pimento
1 tablespoon chopped parsley
1 teaspoon grated onion, fine
½ teaspoon salt

Cook the gluten macaroni according to directions on the package. Drain and rinse. Blend hot milk with breadcrumbs, add ¾ cup grated cheese. Cover until the cheese melts, then add macaroni, beaten egg yolks, pimento, parsely, onion, and salt. Fold in the freshly whipped egg whites. Pour into a shallow flat baking dish. Set baking dish into a large shallow pan of water. Bake for 35 to 45 minutes in a 350-degree oven, until set. Top with remaining ¼ cup grated cheese and return to the oven until cheese is melted.

Serves 4. (293 calories per serving.)

EGGS FLORENTINE

2 cups chopped cooked spinach, drained
6 eggs
1 can Claybourne Dietetic Condensed Cream of Mushroom Soup
1 cup shredded American cheese

Spread spinach over bottom of a shallow casserole, making 6 indentations for the eggs. Break an egg into each. Heat the undiluted soup together with ¾ cup grated cheese. Pour this mixture around the eggs and sprinkle with the remaining ¼ cup cheese. Bake for about 30 minutes in a 350-degree oven.

Serves 6. (177 calories per serving.)

DEVILED EGGS

4 hard boiled eggs
1 tablespoon Loeb Dietetic Mayonnaise
1 teaspoon prepared mustard
¼ teaspoon salt
Dash of paprika

Slice eggs in half, lengthwise. Scoop egg yolk out carefully. Blend yolks with mayonnaise, mustard and salt. Pile back into the whites, swirling the surface with a fork. Sprinkle with a dash of paprika.

40 calories in each deviled egg half.

POACHED EGGS ON ASPARAGUS

2 cups boiling water
1 tablespoon vinegar
¼ teaspoon Sucaryl
½ teaspoon salt

4 eggs
1 (8 ounce) can S & W Nutra-diet Pack Asparagus Points

Add vinegar, Sucaryl and salt to the briskly boiling water. Crack open eggs, 1 at a time, and slip each into the briskly boiling water. Poach for 3 minutes. Remove from water with a slotted spoon, and serve on drained asparagus points.

Serves 2. (170 calories per serving.)

TUNA PUFF

1 can Mott's Figure Control Tuna Newburg
2 eggs, separated
⅛ teaspoon salt
    Pinch of cayenne

Heat Tuna Newburg and stir in lightly beaten egg yolks and cayenne. Beat egg whites stiffly with salt; fold into tuna mixture. Bake in a 1-quart casserole, 400 degrees F. for about 15 minutes.

Serves 4. 114 calories each. (236 calories a serving with regular tuna Newburg.)

Chapter Ten

DIETER'S DESSERTS

Who wants to skip dessert? It's like leaving the theater after the second act, and hungrily wondering what happened in act three.

A sweet-tasting dessert does not have to be loaded with calories to rate a round of applause as the curtain falls on the dinner hour.

It can be a simple gelatin dessert, or an unusual gelatin dessert combined with dietetic fruit.

It can be a tray of dietetic cookies, or a more complicated low-calorie cake.

It can be dietetic ice cream with low-calorie sauce.

Or it can be any one of the many recipes in this chapter, specially devised to give your low-calorie meal a surprise ending.

APPLE, APRICOT AND GRAPE BON-BONNETTES

APPLE BON-BONNETTES

3 large apples, pared, cored and sliced
1 tablespoon lemon juice
2½ teaspoons Adolph's Granulated Sugar Substitute
2 envelopes unflavored gelatin
½ cup cold water
⅛ teaspoon orange extract
¾ cup coarsely chopped walnuts
2 tablespoons cornstarch
¼ teaspoon Adolph's Granulated Sugar Substitute

Combine apples with lemon juice in a saucepan; cover and cook over low heat until tender. Purée (makes about 1½ cups); mix with 2½ teaspoons Adolph's Granulated Sugar Substitute. Sprinkle gelatin over cold water to soften. Add to apple purée; heat until gelatin is dissolved. Remove from heat; stir in orange extract. Refrigerate, stirring occasionally, until consistency of broken egg white.. Add nuts, blending thoroughly. Pour into wax paper lined 8 x 4-inch pan. Refrigerate until firm.

Invert pan onto board that has been sprinkled with the mixture of 2 tablespoons of cornstarch and ¼ teaspoon Adolph's Granulated Sugar Substitute. Peel off wax paper; cut into ¾ x 1½-inch pieces; roll in remaining cornstarch mixture. Store in refrigerator. Can be kept one week.

Makes 30 pieces. 36 calories per piece.

APRICOT BON-BONNETTES

Substitute apricot purée for apple purée; eliminate lemon juice. (An 8-ounce package of dried apricots cooked with 1½ cups water, and puréed, will yield approximately 1½ cups purée.)

44 calories per piece.

GRAPE BON-BONNETTES

1 12-ounce bottle of unsweetened grape juice
2½ teaspoons Adolph's Granulated Sugar Substitute

2 tablespoons unflavored gelatin
¾ cup cold water
¾ cup chopped walnuts
2 tablespoons cornstarch

Blend grape juice and 2½ teaspoons Adolph's Granulated Sugar Substitute in saucepan. Sprinkle gelatin over cold water to soften. Add to grape juice and heat until gelatin is dissolved. Remove from heat; refrigerate, stirring occasionally, until consistency of unbeaten egg white. Add nuts, blending well.

Pour into wax paper lined 8 x 4-inch pan. Refrigerate until firm. Invert pan onto board that has been sprinkled with mixture of cornstarch and ½ teaspoon of Adolph's Granulated Sugar Substitute. Peel off wax paper. Cut into ¾ x 1½-inch pieces; roll in remaining Adolph's Granulated Sugar Substitute mixture.

32 calories per piece.

APPLE SAUCE COOKIES

1¾ cups cake flour
½ teaspoon salt
1 teaspoon cinnamon
½ teaspoon nutmeg
½ teaspoon cloves
1 teaspoon baking soda
½ cup butter

1 tablespoon Sucaryl solution
1 egg
1 cup S & W Nutradiet Apple Sauce
⅓ cup raisins
1 cup Allbran

Sift together the flour, salt, cinnamon, nutmeg, cloves, and baking soda. Mix butter, Sucaryl and egg until light and fluffy. Then add flour mixture and apple sauce alternately, mixing well after each addition. Fold in raisins and Allbran. Drop by level tablespoonsful onto a greased cookie sheet, about 1-inch apart. Bake in a moderate 375-degree oven for 20 minutes, or until golden brown.

Makes 4 dozen cookies. 39 calories per cookie.

CHOCOLATE-NUT BROWNIES

1 square unsweetened chocolate
⅓ cup butter
2 tablespoons Sucaryl solution
2 teaspoons vanilla
2 eggs, beaten

1 cup sifted cake flour
½ teaspoon salt
½ teaspoon baking soda
¾ cup chopped walnuts

Melt the unsweetened chocolate and butter in a saucepan over low heat. Remove from heat. Add Sucaryl, vanilla and the beaten eggs. Stir until well blended. Add sifted cake flour, salt and baking soda. Mix until blended. Stir in the chopped walnuts. Pour into a greased 8-inch square pan. Level batter in pan. Bake in a 325-degree oven for 20 minutes. Cool. Cut into bars.

Makes 32 Brownies. 55 calories each.

CINNAMON COOKIES

5 tablespoons butter
1 cup sifted flour
¼ teaspoon baking powder
2 teaspoons Sucaryl solution
2 teaspoons vanilla
1 tablespoon milk, fruit juice, or coffee
1 teaspoon cinnamon

Cream butter until light and fluffy. Blend in sifted flour and baking power, mixed together. Mix Sucaryl in vanilla and milk (or other liquid). Stir into flour mixture and mix thoroughly. Sprinkle cinnamon over dough and knead in so there is a streaked appearance. Shape dough into balls, about ½ inch in diameter, and arrange on a cookie sheet. Flatten balls with a fork dipped in cold water. Bake in a 375-degree oven for 15 minutes, or until edges are nicely browned.

Makes 30 cookies. 30 calories per cookie.

LEMON COOKIES

½ cup shortening
1 tablespoon Sucaryl solution
1 egg
1 tablespoon water
1 tablespoon lemon juice
1 tablespoon grated lemon peel
1 teaspoon vanilla
½ cup shredded dry coconut
2 cups sifted flour
1 teaspoon baking powder
½ teaspoon salt

Cream shortening in small mixer bowl on high speed. Add Sucaryl, egg, water, lemon juice, lemon peel, and vanilla. Beat until thoroughly blended. Mix in coconut. Sift dry ingredients together; add to creamed mixture, mixing thoroughly. Form dough into a roll, 2 inches in diameter; wrap in waxed paper; chill until firm. Cut into thin slices and bake on an ungreased cookie sheet in a hot oven (400 degrees) for 10 to 15 minutes. Makes 4½ dozen cookies. 35 calories each.

BAKED LEMON CHEESECAKE

4 cups cottage cheese
8 teaspoons Sucaryl solution
1 cup skim milk
8 eggs, slightly beaten
1 teaspoon vanilla

1 tablespoon lemon rind
2 tablespoons lemon juice
2 tablespoons graham cracker crumbs

Place cottage cheese in large bowl of mixer; beat on high speed until smooth and creamy. Blend in Sucaryl, milk, and eggs; beat until smooth. Add vanilla, lemon rind and juice. Pour into a 9-inch spring form pan which has been sprinkled with graham cracker crumbs. Bake in a slow oven (325 degrees) for 1 hour and 15 minutes, or until set.

Serves 12. (133 calories per serving.)

CHOCOLATE CHEESE LOAF

2 tablespoons unflavored gelatin
¼ teaspoon salt
½ cup cocoa
3 tablespoons Sucaryl solution
2 eggs, separated

1 cup skim milk
3 cups skim-milk cottage cheese, sieved
1 teaspoon vanilla
⅓ cup non-fat dry milk
⅓ cup iced water

Lightly grease an 11 x 4 x 2-inch loaf pan. Place gelatin, salt and cocoa in top of double boiler. Combine Sucaryl, egg yolks and milk; blend into dry ingredients. Cook over boiling water, stirring constantly, until mixture thickens (about 10 minutes). Remove from heat. Stir in sieved cottage cheese and vanilla. Chill until mixture begins to mound. Beat egg whites until peaks form. Fold into gelatin mixture.

Combine dry milk and iced water, beating on high speed of mixer until of consistency of whipped cream. Fold into gelatin mixture. Turn into prepared loaf pan. Chill until firm. Unmold and garnish, if desired, with low-calorie whipped topping and shaved unsweetened chocolate.

Serves 12. (105 calories per serving.)

CHOCOLATE CHIFFON CAKE

2 cups flour
½ cup sugar
3 tablespoons Mott's Figure Control Powder Sweetener
2 teaspoons baking soda
1 teaspoon salt
½ cup salad oil

7 eggs, separated
1 (5 ounce) jar Mott's Figure Control Chocolate Topping
1 teaspoon almond extract
¾ cup cold water
½ teaspoon cream of tartar
1 tablespoon vinegar

Sift dry ingredients into a bowl. Make a well in center and add salad oil, egg yolks, chocolate topping and almond extract. Beat gradually adding water, until smooth, then beat stiff and dry. Beat in vinegar. Fold egg whites into chocolate mixture gradually, cutting mixture carefully until blended. Pour into ungreased 10-inch tube pan and bake in a 325-degree oven for 80 minutes. Reduce temperature to 250 degrees and bake 50 minutes longer to dry out. Invert cake on an empty soda bottle or other narrow-necked holder so that air can circulate over and under. Allow to cool completely. Run a knife blade around edges, turn out.

Serves 20. 137 calories per serving. (Regular chocolate chiffon cake is 194 calories per serving.)

CHOCOLATE SPONGE ROLL

5 eggs
5 teaspoons Sucaryl solution
1 tablespoon lemon juice
2 teaspoons vanilla
¼ teaspoon red food coloring

¾ cup sifted cake flour
¼ cup sifted cocoa
¼ teaspoon salt
¼ teaspoon baking soda

Beat eggs in large mixer bowl on high speed until light, 5 minutes. Add Sucaryl, lemon juice, vanilla and food coloring. Continue beating on high speed until stiff peaks form, 10 minutes. Sift dry ingredients together 3 times. Gradually blend in cocoa-flour mixture on low speed, 2 minutes. Line bottom of jelly-roll pan (15½ x 10½ x 1-inches) with well oiled waxed paper. Pour in batter. Smooth top. Bake in a 300-degree oven for 20 minutes, or until top springs back when lightly touched. Turn onto a sheet of waxed paper, sifted with 1 tablespoon cornstarch and 8 crushed Sucaryl tablets. Peel paper from bottom of cake. Trim off crisp edges. Roll up cake with waxed paper until cool. Unwrap and spread with filling; then rewrap and place in refrigerator for at least 2 hours before serving.

CREAM FILLING:

2 tablespoons cornstarch	1½ teaspoons Sucaryl solution
¼ teaspoon salt	1 egg yolk, slightly beaten
1 cup water	¼ teaspoon vanilla
1 tablespoon cream	

Put cornstarch and salt in saucepan; add water; stir until smooth. Add cream and Sucaryl. Cook over medium heat until mixture comes to a boil and is medium thick, stirring constantly. Mix a small amount of the sauce with egg yolk, and return to saucepan. Cook about 3 minutes longer until well thickened. Stir in vanilla. Cool. Spread on chocolate sponge roll. Reroll.

Serves 12. (74 calories per serving.)

COFFEE SPONGE CAKE

5 eggs, separated	1½ cups sifted cake flour
3 tablespoons Sucaryl solution	½ teaspoon baking powder
1 tablespoon lemon juice	¼ teaspoon salt
½ cup strong coffee	¾ teaspoon cream of tartar

Preheat oven to 325 degrees. Beat egg yolks until thick and lemon-colored; add Sucaryl, lemon juice and coffee; beat on high speed of mixer until thick and fluffy, about 10 minutes. Sift together flour, baking powder and salt; carefully fold into egg yolk mixture. Beat egg whites until foamy; add cream of tartar and beat until stiff peaks form when beater is raised. Fold egg yolk mixture gently into whites; pour into a 9-inch tube pan. Bake in preheated oven (325 degrees), 45 to 50 minutes.

Serves 12. (78 calories per serving.)

DESSERT TOPPING

Prepare Dream Whip Dessert Topping Mix with cold strong coffee or with reconstituted non-fat dry milk, instead of cold milk. Or use ¾-cup Cola or ginger ale low-calorie beverage instead of the cold milk and vanilla.

Calorie count for Dream Whip Dessert Topping Mix, made by General Foods Corporation:

About 10 calories per tablespoon with coffee.
About 11 calories per tablespoon with dietetic ginger ale.
About 13 calories per tablespoon with skim milk.
About 14 calories per tablespoon with whole milk.

MARMALADE CAKE

2 cups sifted cake flour
3 teaspoons baking powder
¼ teaspoon salt
⅓ cup soft butter
¾ cup skim milk

4 teaspoons Sucaryl solution
4 drops yellow food coloring
⅓ cup egg whites (about 2)
1 8-ounce jar Louis Sherry
    Dietetic Orange Marmalade

Sift cake flour, baking powder and salt into a small mixer bowl. Add butter and cut in on low speed. Combine milk, Sucaryl and coloring. Add all but ¼ cup of this liquid; beat ½ minute on medium speed. Add remaining liquid; beat 1 minute more. Add unbeaten egg whites; beat 1 minute (mixture will have a curdled appearance). Pour into an 8-inch round aluminum cake pan lined with greased waxed paper. Bake in a 375-degree oven about 20 minutes. Cool 10 minutes before removing from pan. To serve, cut cake in half making 2 semicircles. Put together as a layer cake, using marmalade for filling and topping.

Serves 12. 118 calories per serving.

SPONGE CAKE

7 eggs, separated
½ cup cold water
3 tablespoons Sucaryl solution
½ teaspoon vanilla

2 tablespoons lemon juice
¾ teaspoon cream of tartar
1½ cups sifted cake flour
¼ teaspoon salt

Beat egg yolks until thick and lemon-colored; add combined water, Sucaryl, vanilla and lemon juice mixture to egg yolks; beat until thick and fluffy. Beat whites until foamy; add cream of tartar and beat until stiff peaks form. Fold carefully into yolk mixture. Combine sifted flour and salt; sift a little at a time over the mixture, folding in gently. Pour into an ungreased 9- or 10-inch tube pan. Bake in a slow oven (325 degrees) for 1 hour and 15 minutes.

Serves 12. (91 calories per serving.)

SPONGE CAKE ROLL

3 eggs
½ cup sugar
1 tablespoon Mott's Figure Control Powder Sweetener
⅓ cup water
1 teaspoon vanilla

1 cup flour
1 teaspoon baking powder
¼ teaspoon salt
1 tablespoon confectioners' sugar

Line a 15½ x 10-inch jelly-roll pan with aluminum foil and grease the foil lightly. Beat eggs until very thick and light. Gradually beat in sugar and sweetener and the liquids. Sift the flour, baking powder, and salt together and sift gradually into the batter, beating until the mixture is blended. Pour the batter into the prepared pan and bake the cake in a 375-degree oven for 10-12 minutes, until cake is golden brown and springs back when lightly touched.

Meanwhile, place a dry tea towel atop a dampened one, on a flat surface. Sprinkle dry towel with one tablespoon confectioners' sugar. Turn the baked cake out on the sugared towel at once when removed from oven. Carefully peel off the foil. Trim the crisp edges, and while the cake is still warm roll it from the narrow end, lifting the roll with the aid of the towel. Cool the roll on a wire rack. Unroll the cake and spread it with any of the fillings below. Roll up again.

Makes 10 servings. Without filling, the cake has 105 calories per serving.

CHERRY ROLL

Unroll cooked sponge-cake roll, spread with one cup chilled Mott's Figure Control Cherries in Sauce, and roll again. Spoon ½ cup cherries in sauce on top of the roll, allowing it to drip down the sides.

Serves 10. (129 calories per serving.)

CHOCOLATE CREAM ROLL

6 tablespoons non-fat dry milk solids
1 cup cold water
1 envelope unflavored gelatin

1 jar (5½ oz.) Mott's Figure Control Chocolate Topping
2 egg whites
1 tablespoon confectioners' sugar

Dissolve non-fat dry milk solids in ¾ cup cold water; soak gelatin in ¼ cup cold water. Combine the two mixtures and stir over boiling water until the gelatin dissolves. Add chocolate topping. Chill, stirring occasionally, until mixture is thick enough to mound in a spoon. Beat the egg whites stiff and fold in the chocolate mixture. Unroll the jelly-roll cake, spread it with the chocolate cream filling, and roll up again. Sprinkle with confectioners' sugar. Chill until serving time.

Makes 10 servings, 125 calories per serving. (With regular chocolate cream filling and jelly-roll cake, this would have about 345 calories a serving.)

APPLE MERINGUE

1 jar (1 pound, 7½ ounces) Mott's Figure Control Apple Pie Filling
2 egg whites
    Pinch cream of tartar
2 tablespoons sugar
½ teaspoon Mott's Figure Control Powder Sweetener

Pour apple pie filling into an 8-inch pie plate. Beat egg white with cream of tartar until stiff. Beat in sugar and sweetener. Pour over apples, forming peaks in meringue. Bake at 350 degrees for 20 minutes until golden. Serve warm, or cool and chill for later.

Serves 6. (99 calories per serving.) (Regular would be 243 calories.)

FRUITED MERINGUES

4 egg whites
4 tablespoons sugar
1 teaspoon Mott's Figure Control Powdered Sweetener

Set oven to preheat to 225 degrees. Have egg whites at room temperature. Beat until soft peaks form. Combine sugar and sweetener; fold in gradually. Beat to form stiff peaks. Shape nests using a pastry tube, and place on cookie sheet lined with brown paper. Bake at 225 degrees for 1¾ hours. Turn off oven, leaving meringues to cool in the warm oven. Makes 8.

FILLING:

1 can (12½ oz.) Mott's Figure Control Vanilla Gelatin Custard Dessert

1 cup Mott's Figure Control

Cherry Pie Fillings or other fruits

1 jar (5 oz.) Mott's Figure Control Chocolate Topping

Chill vanilla gelatin custard dessert according to directions on can. Fill each cold meringue with 2 tablespoons of this. Add 1 ounce cherry pie filling, sliced peaches, fruit cocktail, or preserves, or 1 figure control pear half and chocolate topping.

Serves 8. (60 calories per serving.)

APPLE PIE

¾ cup all purpose flour
½ teaspoon salt
1 teaspoon vinegar
3 tablespoons salad oil

1 tablespoon cold milk
1 jar (1 pound, 7½ ounces) Mott's Figure Control Apple Pie Filling

Mix flour and salt. Pour vinegar, then oil, then milk into a small cup and add all at once to flour mixture. Stir to blend, then press into a ball, flatten slightly. Roll out to fit an 8-inch pie plate. Press crust to fit plate, flute edge. Pour in pie filling and bake in 425-degree oven for 25 minutes.

Serves 8. 156 calories per serving. (Regular apple pie has 330 calories.)

CHERRY CHIFFON TARTS

Pastry for a 9-inch pie shell
1 tablespoon unflavored gelatin
¼ cup cold water
1 1-pound can red sour cherries

2 tablespoons Sucaryl solution
1 tablespoon lemon juice
3 eggs, separated

Dieter's Desserts

Roll out pastry and cut into circles to make 10 small tart shells. Bake in a hot oven (425 degrees) about 12 minutes, or until golden brown. Cool.

Soften gelatin in cold water. Drain cherries; add water to liquid to make ¾ cup. Combine this liquid with Sucaryl, lemon juice and egg yolks in top of double boiler. Cook and stir over hot water until mixture thickens. Remove from heat; add softened gelatin, stirring to dissolve; chill until mixture begins to thicken. Beat egg whites stiff and fold into gelatin with the cherries. Spoon into tart shells; chill until set.

Serves 10. (114 calories per serving.)

CHERRY PIE

¾ cup all purpose flour
½ teaspoon salt
1 teaspoon vinegar
3 tablespoons salad oil

1 tablespoon cold milk
1 jar (1 pound, 7½ ounces) Mott's Figure Control Cherry Pie Filling

Mix flour and salt. Pour vinegar, then oil, then milk into a small cup and add all at once to flour mixture. Stir to blend, then press into a ball, flattening slightly. Roll out to fit an 8-inch pie plate. Press crust to fit plate, flute edge. Pour in pie filling and bake in 425-degree oven for 25 minutes.

Serves 8. 166 calories per serving (compared with 340 calories for regular cherry pie).

CHERRY CUSTARD CRUMB PIE

1 cup corn-flake crumbs
1 teaspoon Mott's Figure Control Non-Caloric Powder Sweetener
1½ tablespoons butter, melted
1½ tablespoons water

1 can (12½ oz.) Figure Control Vanilla Gelatin Custard Dessert
1 cup Figure Control Cherry Pie Filling

Combine crumbs, sweetener, melted butter and water; pour into an 8-inch pie plate. Dampen fingertips in additional water, and press crumb mixture firmly to sides and bottom of pie plate. Bake in a 350-degree oven, 10 minutes. Cool.

Stir vanilla gelatin custard dessert until smooth, and pour into cooled crumb crust. Chill until custard sets, top with cherry pie filling, chill again until serving time.

Serves 8. 120 calories per serving (compared to 237 calories per serving ·of the same pie made with regular foods).

CITRUS CHIFFON PIE

1 tablespoon unflavored gelatin
¼ cup cold water
4 teaspoons Sucaryl solution
⅓ cup unsweetened canned grapefruit-orange juice blend

Dash of salt
3 eggs, separated
1 9-inch baked, cooled pastry shell

Soften gelatin in cold water. In top of double boiler, combine Sucaryl, fruit juice, salt, and egg yolks. Cook over hot (not boiling) water only until mixture coats the spoon. Remove from heat; add softened gelatin, stirring to dissolve. Chill until mixture begins to thicken. Beat egg whites until stiff peaks form; fold into thickened gelatin. Spoon into pastry shell. Chill until set. Garnish with low-calorie whipped topping and orange sections, if desired.

Serves 6. (159 calories per serving.)

COCONUT CUSTARD PIE

2⅔ cups skim milk
5 eggs
1 tablespoon Sucaryl solution
¼ teaspoon salt

1 teaspoon vanilla
Dash of nutmeg
¾ cup toasted coconut, fresh or unsweetened

Scald milk. Combine eggs, Sucaryl, salt and vanilla in a large mixer bowl and blend well. Slowly add the scalded milk and beat slightly. Pour into a well greased 8-inch pie plate. Sprinkle with nutmeg. Bake in a 450-degree oven for 5 minutes; reduce heat to 350 degrees and bake 15 minutes longer, or until a knife inserted near the center comes out clean. Cool and garnish edge with toasted coconut.

Serves 6. 146 calories per serving.

COFFEE CHARLOTTE

1 tablespoon unflavored gelatin	Dash of salt
1/3 cup cold skim milk	1/4 cup non-fat dry milk
1/2 cup hot strong coffee	1/4 cup ice water
1 tablespoon Sucaryl solution	9 ladyfingers, split
1 egg white	

Soften gelatin in cold milk. Add hot coffee and Sucaryl, stirring to dissolve gelatin. Chill until mixture begins to thicken. Beat egg white and salt until peaks form. Fold into gelatin.

Combine dry milk and ice water; beat on high speed of mixer until of consistency of whipped cream. Fold into gelatin mixture. Chill until mixture begins to get firm. Line 6 sherbet glasses with 3 split ladyfingers in each. Fill with gelatin mixture. Chill until set.

Serves 6. (64 calories per serving.)

COFFEE EGGNOG PIE

16 small graham crackers, crushed	1/2 cup cold water
3/4 teaspoon Sucaryl solution	4 tablespoons instant coffee
3 tablespoons melted butter	2 cups boiling water
2 tablespoons unflavored gelatin	1 tablespoon brandy flavoring
1 tablespoon Sucaryl solution	2 eggs, separated
	1/2 cup evaporated milk, chilled

Combine crushed graham crackers, 3/4 teaspoon of Sucaryl and the melted butter. Press into a 9-inch pie plate. Chill until firm. Soften gelatin in cold water. Dissolve coffee in boiling water;

add to softened gelatin, stirring to dissolve. Add the 1 tablespoon of Sucaryl. Slowly pour gelatin mixture over well beaten
egg yolks; chill until mixture begins to thicken. Beat egg whites
until peaks form; fold into gelatin mixture along with the flavor-
ing. Beat chilled evaporated milk until stiff; fold into the gelatin
mixture. Pour into crumb crust. Chill until firm. If desired,
garnish with low-caloried whipped topping.

Serves 6. (152 calories per serving.)

CRANBERRY-ORANGE TARTS

Pastry for 9-inch pie shell
2 cups cranberries
½ cup orange juice
½ cup water
3 tablespoons Sucaryl solution

1 tablespoon cornstarch
1 tablespoon unflavored gelatin
¼ cup cold water
1 cup orange sections

Cut pastry into circle to fit 10 small tart pans. Bake in a
hot oven (425 degrees) for 12 minutes, or until golden brown;
cool. Combine cranberries, orange juice and water; cook until
skins pop. Force through sieve. Add Sucaryl to pulp. Combine
a little of the fruit mixture with cornstarch to make a smooth
paste. Return to fruit mixture. Cook, stirring constantly until
thick. Soften gelatin in cold water; add hot fruit mixture,
stirring to dissolve gelatin. Chill until almost set. Spoon into
tart shells; top with orange sections.

Makes 10 servings. 96 calories per serving.

CHOCOLATE CUSTARD TARTLETS

PASTRY:

1½ cups all-purpose flour
1 teaspoon salt
2 teaspoons vinegar

6 tablespoons salad oil
2 tablespoons cold milk

FILLING:

1 can (12½ oz.) Mott's Figure Control Chocolate Gelatin Custard Dessert
Mott's Figure Control Pineapple Tidbits, Pineapple Topping, Fruit Cocktail, Apricot Halves, and Chocolate Topping.
Whipped dessert Topping

Mix flour and salt. Pour vinegar, then oil, then milk into a cup and add all at once to flour mixture. Stir to blend, then press into a ball; divide ball in 10 equal portions. Press each portion into a ball, flatten slightly. Place between two sheets of waxed paper. Dampen table top to prevent slipping, and roll pastry to fit tiny tart shell or muffin cup. Peel off wax paper and lay pastry on tart pan. Fit over backs of muffin cups or custard cups, making pleats so pastry will fit close, or fit inside individual tart pans. Prick with a fork. Repeat with leftover pastry portions, using scraps to form two more tartlet shells, making 12 in all. Place individual tartlets on baking sheet. Bake in a 475-degree oven for 10 minutes.

To fill, shake chocolate gelatin custard dessert, chill 1 hour, stir until smooth, and spoon into cooled pastry shells. Refrigerate until custard sets. Design your own gay tartlet toppings—crisscrossed pineapple tidbits and a dab of pineapple topping, a fruit cocktail wreath, an apricot half filled with apricot pineapple preserves, any low-calorie whipped dessert topping with dribbles of chocolate topping.

Makes 1 dozen tartlets, averaging 144 calories each.

LEMON CHIFFON PIE

1 tablespoon unflavored gelatin
¼ cup lemon juice
2 teaspoons grated lemon rind
4 egg whites
2 egg yolks
¼ cup water
¼ teaspoon salt
5 teaspoons Sucaryl solution
¼ cup cake flour
¾ cup boiling water
½ cup non-fat dry milk solids
½ cup iced water
⅛ teaspoon yellow food coloring
¼ cup fine toasted breadcrumbs

Mix gelatin with lemon juice and rind. Beat egg whites until soft peaks form. Beat egg yolks with water, salt, Sucaryl, and flour until blended. Add boiling water. Pour mixture into a saucepan and bring to boil rapidly. Stir vigorously as mixture thickens, about 1 minute. Remove from heat. Add softened gelatin immediately, stirring until blended. Fold beaten egg whites into lemon mixture. Brush 9-inch pie plate with oil. Sprinkle with crumbs, coating sides and bottom of plate. Pour in lemon mixture. Chill until firm.

For low-calorie topping, add ½ cup non-fat dry milk solids to ½ cup ice water and 1 teaspoon Sucaryl. Beat on high speed until of consistency of whipped cream. Spread on pie.

Serves 8. (102 calories per serving.)

RASPBERRY CHIFFON PIE

1 tablespoon gelatin
¼ cup cold water
3 eggs, separated
4 teaspoons Sucaryl solution

⅛ teaspoon salt
1 tablespoon lemon juice
2 cups fresh red raspberries
1 9-inch baked pie shell

Soften gelatin in cold water; dissolve over boiling water. Combine egg yolks, Sucaryl, salt and lemon juice; beat on high speed of mixer until light and pale in color.

Crush and strain ½ cup of the raspberries. Add slowly to the egg mixture in the top of a double boiler; cook, stirring constantly, until slightly thickened. Stir in dissolved gelatin; chill until mixture begins to set. Beat egg whites until stiff peaks form; fold into thickened gelatin along with the remaining berries. Pour into baked pie shell; chill until set.

Serves 8. (102 calories per serving.)

APRICOT WHIP

1 envelope orange D-Zerta
½ cup hot water
½ cup canned apricot juice
1½ teaspoons lemon juice

⅛ teaspoon rum extract (optional)
½ cup (8-ounce can) chopped drained unsweetened apricots

Dissolve D-Zerta in hot water. Add fruit juices and rum extract. Chill until slightly thickened. Place bowl in iced water. Whip with an egg beater until thick and fluffy. Fold in apricots. Pour into molds and chill.

Serves 3. (31 calories per serving.)

BAKED CUSTARD

2 eggs, lightly beaten
1½ teaspoons Adolph's Granulated Sugar Substitute

2 cups skim milk
1 teaspoon vanilla
Nutmeg

Combine beaten eggs with Adolph's Granulated Sugar Substitute; slowly add skim milk and vanilla, blending well. Pour mixture equally into 4 custard cups; top with a sprinkling of nutmeg. Bake in pan of hot water in a moderate oven (325 degrees) about 1 hour, or until mixture does not adhere to knife.

Serves 4. (82 calories per serving.)

CHOCOLATE CREME

6 tablespoons non-fat dry milk solids
1 cup cold water
1 envelope unflavored gelatin
1 (5 ounce) jar Mott's Figure Control Chocolate Topping
2 egg whites

Dissolve non-fat dry milk solid in ¾ cup of cold water; soak gelatin in remaining ¼ cup of water. Combine and heat over boiling water until gelatin dissolves. Add chocolate topping. Cool until liquid mounds in a spoon. Beat egg whites; fold in chocolate mixture. Spoon into dessert glasses and chill.

Serves 8. 25 calories per serving (regular chocolate pots de crème have about 290 calories).

BAKED LEMON PUDDING CAKE

½ cup flour
½ teaspoon baking powder
2 eggs, separated
2 teaspoons grated lemon rind

¼ cup fresh lemon juice
1½ cups skim or nonfat milk
2 teaspoons Adolph's Granulated Sugar Substitute

1. Measure flour and baking powder into sifter; sift together. Beat egg yolks until lemon-colored; add lemon rind and juice, milk and Adolph's Granulated Sugar Substitute; beat thoroughly. Add flour mixture and beat until smooth.

2. Beat egg whites until stiff but not dry, so they stand in peaks; fold into egg yolk mixture. Pour into a lightly oiled 1-quart soufflé or baking dish. Set in pan containing ½-inch hot water. Bake at 350 degrees F. 30 to 35 minutes. Let cool at least 15 minutes before serving. Pudding will separate into cake layer and sauce layer.

Serves 6. Granulated sugar substitute recipe, 82 calories per serving.

VALENTINE'S ANGEL CAKE

7 eggs, separated
4½ teaspoons Adolph's Granulated Sugar Substitute
⅔ cup cold water
½ teaspoon vanilla

3 tablespoons lemon juice
1 teaspoon lemon extract
¾ teaspoon cream of tartar
1½ cups sifted cake flour
¼ teaspoon salt

1. Preheat oven to 325 degrees F. Line 2 heart-shaped layer cake pans (8 inch) with wax paper.

2. Beat egg yolks until thick and lemon-colored, about five minutes, adding Adolph's Granulated Sugar Substitute during the last minute of beating.

3. Combine water, vanilla, lemon juice and lemon extract;

add to egg yolk mixture; beat until thick and fluffy, about 10 minutes.

4. Beat egg whites until foamy; add cream of tartar; beat until stiff, glossy peaks form. Fold into yolk mixture.

5. Sift about ¼ of the flour mixture at a time over the egg mixture, folding in gently until all flour disappears. (Use 15 folding strokes for each addition.)

6. Pour batter into prepared pans; spread evenly. Bake at 325 degrees F. 30 to 35 minutes.

Variation: If you do not have heart-shaped pans, you can make a one-layer heart-shaped cake using one 8-inch square pan and one 8-inch round pan. When layers are done, cut the round one in half and place the halves against two adjoining sides of the square layer. Then carefully trim the V of the heart to make a perfect heart shape.

WHIPPED ANGEL TOPPING

¼ cup instant nonfat dry milk
⅛ teaspoon Adolph's
    Granulated Sugar Substitute
¼ cup ice water
¼ teaspoon vanilla
1 tablespoon lemon juice
¾ teaspoon unflavored gelatin
1 to 2 drops red food color

1. Soak gelatin in one tablespoon water 5 minutes and dissolve over hot water.

2. Combine all remaining ingredients in small bowl of electric mixer. Beat on high speed about 5 minutes.

3. Add dissolved gelatin very gradually, continuing to beat another few minutes until frosting stands in peaks.

4. Frost cake layers and outer surfaces.

Serves 12. 103 calories per slice (including whipped angel topping).

COFFEE CUSTARD PUDDING

⅓ cup flour
2 tablespoons instant coffee
¼ teaspoon salt
2 cups skim milk, scalded

4½ teaspoons Sucaryl solution
2 eggs, slightly beaten
1 teaspoon vanilla

In the top of a double boiler, combine flour, coffee and salt; slowly add scalded milk to make a smooth sauce. Add Sucaryl and eggs, blending well. Cook in top of double boiler, stirring constantly until thick, about 10 minutes. Remove from heat; cool; add vanilla. Pour into serving dish or individual dessert dishes, and chill. If desired, serve with mounds of whipped dietetic topping, garnished with toasted, slivered almonds.

Serves 5. (92 calories per serving.)

COLD APRICOT SOUFFLE

1 (15 ounce) jar Mott's Figure
  Control Apricot Halves
1 envelope unflavored gelatin
1 (8 ounce) jar Mott's Figure
  Control Apricot-pineapple
  Preserves

4 egg whites
2 tablespoons lemon juice
  Toasted almond slivers
  (optional)

Reserve ¼ cup syrup and 10 apricot halves from jar; purée remaining halves, using a sieve or blender. Soften gelatin in reserved syrup. Stir puréed apricots, softened gelatin and preserves over boiling water to dissolve gelatin. Chill until mixture mounds in spoon. Beat egg whites to form stiff peaks, add lemon juice and continue beating until quite stiff. Fold in thickened apricot mixture; pour into 1¼-quart soufflé dish which has been collared* or in 1¾-quart bowl. Chill at least 4 hours.

* So that the soufflé will stand above the rim, tear foil long enough to wrap around outside upper edge of dish with an overlap. Double lengthwise, oil lightly and tie securely around soufflé dish to stand 2 inches above top.

Garnish with reserved apricot halves and toasted almond slivers, if desired.

Serves 8. 48 calories per serving. (Regular, about 207 calories per serving.)

CRANBERRY FLUFF

2 cups cranberries
1 cup water
2 tablespoons Sucaryl solution

2 envelopes D-Zerta Orange Gelatin
1/4 cup non-fat dry milk
1/4 cup iced water

Combine cranberries, water and Sucaryl; cook until skins pop. Drain, saving both liquid and berries. Add enough water to liquid to make 1½ cups; stir in gelatin until dissolved. Chill until mixture begins to set; then beat until frothy. Combine dry milk and iced water; beat on high speed of mixer until of consistency of whipped cream; fold into gelatin mixture. Fold in cooked cranberries. Chill until mixture just begins to set. Pile into sherbets or parfaits.

Serves 6. (42 calories per serving.)

FRENCH PEACH CREAM

½ cup sour cream
4½ teaspoons Sucaryl solution
½ teaspoon salt
½ teaspoon vanilla
¼ teaspoon almond extract
1 egg

1 tablespoon unflavored gelatin
¼ cup cold water
¼ cup non-fat dry milk
¼ cup iced water
2 cups sliced fresh peaches
2 tablespoons graham cracker crumbs

Combine sour cream, Sucaryl, salt, vanilla, almond extract and egg; beat well. Soften gelatin in cold water; dissolve over boiling water. Add to sour cream mixture; chill until slightly thickened. Combine dry milk and iced water; beat on high speed of mixer until of consistency of whipped cream; fold into gelatin mixture. Carefully fold in 1 cup sliced peaches. Spread cracker crumbs over bottom of a shallow baking dish; spoon in gelatin mixture; chill until set. Garnish with remaining peach slices.

Serves 6. (106 calories per serving.)

GRAPE BAVARIAN

   1 envelope lemon D-Zerta
   ½ cup hot water
   ½ cup unsweetened grape juice
   ⅓ cup evaporated milk, chilled until partially frozen
   2 teaspoons lemon juice

Dissolve D-Zerta in hot water. Add grape juice. Chill until slightly thickened. Beat chilled milk with an egg beater until thick. Add lemon juice and beat until mixture is stiff. Place bowl of D-Zerta in iced water; beat until thick and fluffy. Fold in whipped milk. Pour into molds. Chill.

Serves 6. (46 calories per serving.)

LEMON-FLAVORED RICE MOLD

½ cup rice
½ teaspoon salt
½ cup boiling water
2½ cups skim milk
1 tablespoon unflavored gelatin
¼ cup cold water

4 eggs, separated
2 tablespoons Sucaryl solution
1 tablespoon lemon rind
2 tablespoons lemon juice
1 teaspoon vanilla

In the top of a double boiler, combine rice, salt, and boiling water; bring to a boil and cook about 2 minutes. Add milk and cook over hot water until rice is tender (about 10 minutes). Soften gelatin in cold water. Combine egg yolks, Sucaryl, lemon rind, lemon juice, and vanilla. Slowly add some of the hot rice mixture to the egg yolk mixture; return to double boiler and cook 5 minutes longer, stirring occasionally. Remove from heat;

stir in softened gelatin until dissolved; chill slightly. Beat egg whites until stiff peaks form; fold into rice mixture. Spoon into an 8-cup mold and chill until set. To serve, unmold and garnish with orange slices and green grapes.

Serves 8. (114 calories per serving.)

LEMON SHERRY PUDDING

2 tablespoons flour
½ teaspoon cinnamon
½ teaspoon salt
1 egg plus 2 egg yolks
3 tablespoons sherry

2 tablespoons lemon juice
1 cup skim milk
1½ tablespoons Sucaryl solution
2 eggs whites, stiffly beaten

Combine flour, cinnamon and salt in a small bowl. Combine 1 egg plus 2 egg yolks, sherry, lemon juice, milk and Sucaryl. Add to dry ingredients, beating well. Fold in stiffly beaten egg whites. Pour into a lightly buttered casserole. Set in a pan of hot water and bake in a moderate oven (350 degrees) 25 to 30 minutes. Serve warm or chilled.

Serves 4. (109 calories per serving.)

MOCK EGGNOG PUDDING

1 envelope D-Zerta Vanilla Pudding
1 cup milk
¼ teaspoon rum extract
Sprinkling of nutmeg

Add 1 envelope D-Zerta pudding powder to milk in a small saucepan, stirring until well blended. Heat and stir until the mixture comes to a boil. Remove from heat and add rum extract. Pour into serving dishes. Just before serving, sprinkle with nutmeg.

Serves 2. (95 calories per serving.)

ORANGE PUDDING

1 envelope D-Zerta Vanilla Pudding
¾ cup milk
¼ cup orange juice
1 orange sectioned and diced

Add pudding powder to milk and orange juice in a small saucepan, stirring until well blended. Heat and stir until the mixture comes to the boil. Remove from heat and fold in diced orange. Pour into serving dishes. Cool until set.
Serves 2. (123 calories per serving.)

PYRAMID OF PEARS HELENE

2 jars (15 oz. each) Mott's Figure Control Pear Halves
1 jar (5½ oz.) Mott's Figure Control Chocolate Topping

Arrange pears in a pyramid on serving plate. Chill. At serving time, trickle chocolate topping from the top down over the pears.
Serves 8. 49 calories per serving. (With regular pears and chocolate sauce, this would be 143 calories per serving.)

PEACH WINE CREAM

4 eggs, separated
2 tablespoons Sucaryl solution
1 1-pound can Sucaryl-sweetened sliced peaches, drained and crushed

2 tablespoons lemon juice
½ cup white wine
1 tablespoon unflavored gelatin
½ cup cold water

Combine egg yolks and Sucaryl; beat on high speed of mixer until light and fluffy. Add peach pulp, lemon juice and wine. Cook in top of double boiler until smooth and thick.

Soften gelatin in cold water; add to cooked mixture, stirring to dissolve. Allow to cool, stirring occasionally. When mixture has thickened, beat egg whites until peaks form; fold into gelatin mixture. Spoon into serving dish or into individual sherbets. Garnish with peach slices, if desired.

Serves 8. (79 calories per serving.)

PRUNE CUSTARD

1 envelope D-Zerta Vanilla Pudding
1¼ cups milk
¼ cup sieved prunes

Add pudding powder and prunes to milk in a small saucepan, stirring until well blended. Heat and stir until the mixture comes to the boil. Remove from heat and pour into serving dishes. Chill until set.

Serves 3. (98 calories per serving.)

PRUNE WHIP

½ cup unsweetened prune pulp (1 5-ounce jar strained prunes)
1 teaspoon Adolph's Granulated Sugar Substitute
1 teaspoon vanilla
1 teaspoon lemon juice
1 teaspoon unflavored gelatin
1 tablespoon cold water
2 egg whites

Blend first four ingredients together. Soften gelatin in cold water; then dissolve over hot water in double boiler. Beat egg whites until frothy; add gelatin and beat very stiffly; fold into prune mixture. Pile lightly into custard cups or sherbet glasses and chill thoroughly. If desired, 1 teaspoon of chopped walnuts may be sprinkled over each serving. This will add about 16 calories per serving.

Serves 4. (46 calories per serving.)

HAWAIIAN SHERBET

1 (6 oz.) can frozen orange-
  pineapple juice (unsweetened), thawed
¾ cup apple juice
  (unsweetened)

¾ cup cold water
1½ teaspoons Adolph's
    Granulated Sugar Substitute
¼ cup nonfat dry milk solids

1. Combine liquids; add Adolph's Granulated Sugar Substitute, stirring until dissolved. Blend in nonfat dry milk solids; pour mixture into chilled refrigerator tray and freeze. (Moisten bottom of tray for faster freezing.)

2. Place a mixing bowl and rotary beater or wire whisk in refrigerator to chill.

3. Turn sherbet out into chilled bowl and beat until fluffy, but not melted; return at once to refrigerator tray and continue to freeze until almost set; then repeat beating procedure. Keep in freezer compartment until needed.

Serves 8. (63 calories per serving.)

Variation:

Strawberry Sherbet: Omit orange-pineapple juice, apple juice and water. Substitute 1 pint fresh strawberries, hulled and crushed, adding enough cold water to crushed berries to make 2 cups liquid. Add 1 teaspoon lemon juice. Add Adolph's Granulated Sugar Substitute to this mixture and proceed with basic recipe.

Serves 8. (31 calories per serving.)

RASPBERRY SHERBET

4 cups fresh red raspberries
1 cup orange juice
5 tablespoons Sucaryl solution
2 cups water

Wash raspberries; force through a sieve to remove seeds. Add orange juice, Sucaryl and water; blend well. Pour into 2 ice cube trays and place in the freezer. After about 1 hour, remove to a chilled bowl and beat with an electric mixer until smooth but not melted. Pour back into trays and return to freezer. Repeat beating about every 30 minutes until frozen solid.

Makes 1 quart. Serves 8. 48 calories per serving.

SCOTCH APPLE PUDDING

1 envelope D-Zerta Butterscotch Pudding
¾ cup milk
¼ cup diced peeled apples
½ teaspoon lemon juice

Add pudding powder to milk in a small saucepan, stirring until well blended. Heat and stir until the mixture comes to a boil. Remove from heat and fold in diced apples and lemon juice. Pour into serving dishes. Chill until set.

Serves 2. (105 calories per serving.)

TREASURE ISLAND

1 egg white
1 tablespoon sugar
3 tablespoons sieved prunes
1 envelope D-Zerta Vanilla Pudding
1 cup milk

Beat egg white until foamy, add sugar, and beat until stiff peaks will form. Mix in prunes. Pour into serving dishes. Then make D-Zerta pudding with milk as directed. Pour over prune mixture.

Serves 4. (75 calories per serving.)

Chapter Eleven

NIBBLE NOTHINGS

Since 10 medium potato chips have 110 calories, and whoever stops at 10 anyway, it is important to acquire the knowledge of what group of foods lends itself best to be combined with dietetic foods for low-calorie hors d'oeuvres.

Celery and carrot sticks can readily join the dietetic bread sticks as dippers for mock-fondue.

Raw cauliflower flowerets are delicious as they are, or if dipped into a tasty dressing.

Cucumber is excellent in sticks, slices, plain, or pickled.

Mushrooms are extremely low in calories and may be stuffed and broiled, or used alternately with other foods as tiny kabobs.

Hard boiled eggs may be used in a variety of ways, either stuffed, sliced on dietetic crackers, or chopped with low-calorie mayonnaise.

Shrimps can be dunked into low calorie sauces, marinated in Italian dressing, strung on kabobs with low-calorie pineapple, or served hot in marinara sauce.

Canned asparagus combines well with cottage cheese, pineapple, and paper-thin sliced ham.

Yoghurt makes an interesting base for dips in place of higher caloried sour cream.

If you have a beverage with your appetizer, remember that carbonated water and the low-calorie sodas will add little to your daily calorie count, and a low-calorie ginger ale added to a highball will be 100 calories less than a highball with regular ginger ale.

The recipes in this chapter will help you develop a repertoire of hors d'oeuvres that won't endanger your diet and will delight your weight-watching guests.

BROILED LIVER-STUFFED MUSHROOMS

1 pound large mushrooms (size of a half-dollar)
1 can Mott's Figure Control Chopped Chicken Liver

Remove stems and wash fresh mushroom caps. Fill each center with about ½ teaspoon chopped chicken liver. Arrange on a flat cookie sheet. Broil for 10 minutes, just before serving time.

About 10 calories per mushroom cap.

MUSHROOM PICKUPS

1 can whole mushrooms, drained
1 cup Mott's Figure Control Italian Dressing

Marinate the drained mushrooms in Italian dressing for several hours in the refrigerator. Serve with toothpicks as appetizing pickups.

About 3 calories each.

CHICKEN LIVER KABOBS

12 chicken livers, quartered
24 drained button mushroom caps
48 pieces Libby's Dietetic Pineapple Tidbits
24 long wooden toothpicks

Skewer two pieces of chicken liver and two pineapple tidbits, alternately on each toothpick. Finish each with a mushroom cap. Arrange in a shallow broiling pan and broil for 10 minutes before serving. Serve hot.

Makes 24 kabobs. 23 calories each.

CHEESE DIP

1½ cups cottage cheese   1 teaspoon salt
½ cup Dannon Yoghurt   ½ teaspoon grated lemon rind
1 teaspoon prepared mustard   1 tablespoon chopped chives

Combine all ingredients into a smooth consistency. Use as a dip for raw carrot and raw cauliflower spears.

Makes about 2 cups of dip. 14 calories per tablespoon.

RED CAVIAR DIP

1 cup cottage cheese
1 cup Dannon Yoghurt
1 (2 ounce) jar red caviar
1 teaspoon finely grated onion

Blend the cottage cheese and yoghurt together. Add the red caviar and finely grated onion. Use as a dip.

Makes about 2⅛-cups. 12 calories per tablespoon.

QUICK FONDUE POT

2 cans Mott's Figure Control Welsh Rarebit
2 dozen bread sticks
2 dozen celery sticks

Empty Welsh rarebit into a fondue pot or chafing dish, and set over a burner. Keep warm, for dipping with bread sticks and celery sticks.

39 calories per bread stick dipped in a tablespoon of fondue.
14 calories per celery stick dipped in a tablespoon of fondue.

FRANKFURTER BISCUITS

1 package of brown and serve biscuits (in round tube)
4 frankfurters
4 tablespoons Mott's Figure Control Apricot-pineapple Preserves
2 teaspoons prepared mustard

Open the round tube of biscuits and separate the 10 pieces of prepared dough. Cut each biscuit into four pie-shaped sections. Then slice each frankfurter into 10 slices (about ½ inch each). Press a slice of frankfurter into the center of each biscuit quarter. Arrange on a cookie sheet and bake according to the instructions on the package.

Blend the apricot-pineapple preserves with the prepared mustard and serve as a dip for the frankfurter biscuits.

Makes 40 pieces. 27 calories each, including dip.

FROZEN LANGESTINOS IN SAUCE

1 package cooked frozen langestinos (3 dozen)
½ cup Loeb Dietetic Mayonnaise
4 tablespoons ketchup
6 stuffed olives, chopped fine
¼ teaspoon salt
1 teaspoon white horse-radish
½ teaspoon sugar

Thaw langestinos. Blend remaining ingredients together. Mix through langestinos, coating them generously. Serve with a toothpick through each langestino.

Makes 3 dozen. 12 calories each.

HAM-ASPARAGUS ROLLS

6 slices ham, cut thin and very lean
1 can S & W Nutradiet Asparagus
½ cup cottage cheese, creamy smooth
2 tablespoons chopped chives

Cut each slice of ham in half. Spread thinly with the chives mixed into cottage cheese. Lay a spear of asparagus along one edge and roll up the half ham slice. Cut each roll in half and fasten securely with toothpicks.
Makes 24. 28 calories per roll.

MARINATED SHRIMPS

2 pounds of cooked peeled shrimps
1 bottle Mott's Figure Control Italian Dressing
1 sliced onion
1 clove crushed garlic

Pour Italian dressing into a deep bowl. Add sliced onion and crushed garlic. Add cleaned, cooked shrimps to the marinade and refrigerate for several hours. Serve drained, with toothpicks speared into each shrimp.
About 13 calories per marinated shrimp.

QUICK SHRIMP MARINARA

3 pounds fresh shrimps
1 cup Mott's Figure Control Spaghetti Sauce

Peel and devein shrimps. Bring sauce to a boil, add shrimps. Simmer 2-5 minutes or until tender. Garnish with parsley and lemon wedges.
Makes about 48 shrimps in sauce. 21 calories per shrimp.

MEATBALLS WITH FRUITY SAUCE

2 cans Mott's Figure Control Meatballs in Brown Gravy
4 tablespoons Mott's Figure Control Apricot-pineapple Preserves
2 teaspoons prepared mustard
1 teaspoon lemon juice

Blend the mustard and lemon juice into the preserves. Add to the gravy of the meatballs. Add meatballs, heat and serve with toothpicks speared into each meatball.

About 24 meatballs. 30 calories per meatball.

MEATBALLS WITH HORSE-RADISH SAUCE

2 cans Mott's Figure Control Meatballs in Brown Gravy
2 teaspoons horse-radish
1 teaspoon lemon juice

Blend the horseradish and lemon juice into the gravy of the meatballs. Add meatballs, heat and serve with toothpicks speared into each meatball.

About 24 meatballs. 28 calories per meatball.

PIZZA PICKUPS

4 dozen Diamel Gluten Crackers
1 can Claybourne Tomato Soup, condensed
½ teaspoon oregano
½ teaspoon powdered garlic
1 cup grated American Cheddar-type cheese

Blend garlic and oregano into tomato soup. Spread on crackers, top with grated cheese. Sprinkle extra oregano on top as desired. Bake on a cookie sheet for 5 minutes at 400 degrees. Serve hot.

Makes 4 dozen miniature pizza pickups. 16 calories each.

Chapter Twelve

BONUS BREADS

What is home-baked bread doing in a dietetic cookbook? It is importantly rounding out the concept of dining graciously and completely. Why be denied the fragrance and eating pleasure of the traditional staff of life, when a slice of delicious bread will provide the satisfaction and will power to adhere to your well-intentioned resolutions.

Included in this bonus chapter are nine interesting variations of an uncomplicated low-sodium, herb-bread recipe. Not only will it create loaves of appetizing bread, but also can be used for fancy rolls too. The tea-bread recipes can accompany a salad, or substitute for a dessert course.

Are griddle cakes a favorite of yours? By using a specially prepared mix, you can treat yourself to hot golden circles of delectable pancakes for the debit of 56 calories each. Serve with a low-calorie maple mix and you will have sacrificed nothing but calories!

Do enjoy the little extras in dining, while you eat your low-calorie way to slimness!

LOW-SODIUM HERB BREAD

1 cup scalded milk—fat milk
6 tablespoons soft shortening
3 tablespoons sugar
2½ teaspoons Adolph's Seasoned Salt Substitute
1 package active dry yeast, or

1 cake compressed yeast
1 cup very warm water
⅓ cup chopped fresh parsley, chives, or green onion tops
⅛ teaspoon crumbled rosemary
6 cups all-purpose flour

Into scalded milk, stir shortening, sugar and Adolph's Seasoned Salt Substitute. Cool until lukewarm. Sprinkle or crumble yeast into very warm water in large bowl (for compressed yeast, use lukewarm water). Stir until dissolved. Stir in lukewarm milk mixture, parsley and rosemary. Add 3 cups flour. Beat with spoon until smooth. Stir in remaining 3 cups flour. If dough is still too moist to handle, work in a little more flour.

Turn onto lightly floured surface; knead until smooth and elastic. Place in greased bowl; brush lightly with salad oil. Cover with towel; let rise in warm place (about 85 degrees) until double in bulk, about 1½ hours. Punch down; turn rounded side up; cover; let rise in warm place a second time for about 30 minutes (the second rising is not necessary, but produces a better-textured, finer loaf).

Knead well again. Divide dough into 2 portions; mold into a loaf; place in two greased 9 x 5 x 3-inch loaf pans. Brush with salad oil if you wish a soft crust (and can afford the extra calories).

Cover with towel. Set in warm place and let rise until sides of dough have reached top of pan and center is well rounded above pan.

Bake at 400 degrees about 30 minutes, or until done. Remove from pans to rack at once. (If soft crust is desired, cover bread with damp towel for 5 minutes. Wrap when cooled, so loaves won't dry out.)

Makes 20 slices. 84 calories per slice.

NOTE: The sodium content will be reduced even more if

distilled water is used in place of ordinary water. The sodium content will be increased if sweet butter or unsalted margarine is used in place of soft vegetable shortenings.

FOR WHITE BREAD: Use Adolph's Salt Substitute, instead of Adolph's Seasoned Salt Substitute. Omit parsley and rosemary.

VARIATIONS: Make the following rolls and variety shapes with either the herb or white bread doughs:

SWIRL BREAD: Divide dough into 3 portions. Cut one portion in half; roll each half into a 24-inch strip. Twist strip; wind into a coil in center of an 8- or 9-inch round layer pan, well greased with shortening. Twist second strip and coil around first strip. Use the remaining portions of dough for 2 more swirl breads. Let rise to double its bulk; bake at 350 degrees for 35 to 45 minutes.

Makes 12 slices. 93 calories per slice.

FRENCH BRAID BREAD: Use ½ or ⅓ dough, depending on the size braid you wish. Roll into rectangle, ½ inch thick. Cut into 4 strips about 12 inches long; place on greased baking sheet or in shallow greased baking dish. Braid strips together, sealing ends. Sprinkle lightly with sesame seeds. Let rise and bake at 375 degrees about 25 minutes.

Makes 12 slices. 93 calories per slice.

COCKTAIL LOAF: Using about ¼ dough, shape into long, slender roll about 15 inches long. Slash top at 3-inch intervals with sharp knife; sprinkle top with Adolph's Seasoned Salt Substitute. Place seam side down on greased cookie sheet. Curve ends in to form crescent, or make "snail" shape if you wish variety. Let rise and bake at 375 degrees for 20 minutes.

Makes 10 slices. 84 calories per slice.

QUICK CLOVERLEAF ROLLS: Shape dough into 2-inch balls. Place in greased muffin cups; brush with oil. Let rise and bake at 400 degrees about 15 to 20 minutes.

Makes 3 dozen. 93 calories each.

PARKER HOUSE ROLLS: Roll out dough on floured surface to about ¼-inch thickness. Cut into 3-inch rounds, with biscuit cutter. Brush with melted shortening. Mark a crease with dull edge of knife to one side of center of each round. Fold so top half slightly overlaps; press edges together at crease. Place close together on greased baking sheet. Let rise and bake at 400 degrees about 15 to 20 minutes.

Makes 3 dozen. 93 calories each.

HERB STICKS: Roll herb bread dough ½ inch thick. Cut into 6 x ½-inch strips. Pinch each strip into pencil-like shape. Then place fingers on ends of each strip; gently roll strip back and forth, moving fingers to center, then out to ends again, to form evenly shaped 10 x ⅜-inch stick. Place sticks 1 inch apart on greased cookie sheet. Slash tops in 2 places; sprinkle tops with Adolph's Seasoned Salt Substitute. Let rise and bake at 400 degrees about 15 to 20 minutes.

Makes 3 dozen. 93 calories each.

DINNER BRAIDS: Roll out dough to ½-inch thickness. Cut into 5 x ½-inch strips. Braid strips together in groups of 3, sealing ends. Place on greased baking sheets; sprinkle with sesame, caraway or poppy seeds, if desired. Let rise and bake at 400 degrees about 12 to 15 minutes.

Makes 2 dozen. 139 calories each.

BANANA-NUT BREAD

1 pound ripe bananas (3 or 4), mashed	1¾ cups cake flour
	3 teaspoons baking powder
1 tablespoon Adolph's Granulated Sugar Substitute	¼ teaspoon salt
	¼ cup chopped walnuts
2 eggs, well beaten	

Sprinkle Adolph's Granulated Sugar Substitute over bananas and stir until dissolved; blend in eggs. Sift together flour, baking powder and salt; add walnuts; blend thoroughly into banana mixture, but do not overmix. Preheat oven to 350 degrees. Pour butter into greased 4 x 7-inch loaf pan; bake 25 minutes, then reduce heat to 300 degrees and continue baking until done, 35 to 40 minutes.

20 slices per loaf. 59 calories per slice.

CASSEROLE RAISIN BREAD

2 cups biscuit mix
⅓ cup dry oatmeal
1 teaspoon baking powder
¼ teaspoon salt

½ cup raisins
1 egg, well beaten
1¼ cups skim milk
4½ teaspoons Sucaryl solution

Combine biscuit mix, oatmeal, baking powder, salt and raisins. Combine remaining ingredients; add to dry ingredients all at once, blending well. Pour into a lightly greased 1-quart round casserole. Bake in a moderate oven (350 degrees) 50 to 60 minutes. Cool in casserole 10 minutes; turn out on rack for remainder of cooling.

Makes 20 slices. 78 calories per slice.

CHERRY-NUT BREAD

2 cups biscuit mix
26 maraschino cherries, drained, and chopped
¼ cup chopped walnuts

1¼ cups skim milk
2 tablespoons Sucaryl solution
1 egg, well beaten

In a large bowl, combine biscuit mix, cherries and nuts. Combine remaining ingredients; add to dry ingredients all at once, beating well. Pour into 2 nut bread pans. Bake in a moderate oven (350 degrees) 40 to 50 minutes.

Makes 24 slices. 65 calories per slice.

ORANGE TEA RING

2 cups sifted flour
1 teaspoon baking soda
¼ teaspoon salt
1 tablespoon grated orange rind

2 tablespoons Sucaryl solution
1 egg, well beaten
1 cup orange juice
⅓ cup salad oil

Combine flour, baking soda, salt and orange rind. Combine all liquids, and stir into flour all at once, blending well. Pour into a greased 8-inch ring mold. Bake in a slow oven (325 degrees) 40 to 50 minutes.

Makes 20 slices. 81 calories per slice.

MUFFINS

¾ cup Loeb's Dietetic Prepared Mix
½ cup water
¼ teaspoon salt
1 egg
6 quarter-grain saccharin tablets or 5 drops Loeb's Sweetener

Preheat oven to 375 degrees. Dissolve saccharin in water. Stir egg and water together. Add salt. Sift prepared mix. Stir liquid into the mix. When batter is smooth, pour into 4 muffin cups, filling each only half full. Bake for 30 minutes at 375 degrees.

Makes 4. (79 calories per muffin.)

APPLE MUFFINS

1⅔ cups all-purpose flour
2 teaspoons Adolph's Granulated Sugar Substitute
2½ teaspoons baking powder
½ teaspoon salt
1 teaspoon cinnamon
¼ teaspoon nutmeg
1 egg, slightly beaten
⅔ cup skim or nonfat milk
¼ cup melted shortening
1 cup finely chopped apples (approx. 2 medium)

1. Sift flour, Granulated Sugar Substitute, baking powder, salt and spices into mixing bowl.

2. Combine egg, milk and shortening; add to dry ingredients, blend until flour is moistened. Do not overmix; batter should be lumpy.

3. Fold in chopped apples.

4. Line muffin pans or custard cups with paper baking cups; pour batter in ⅔ full; bake at 400 degrees F., 20 to 25 minutes. If paper liners are not used, grease the muffin cups.

Makes 1 dozen. (97 calories each.)

GRIDDLE CAKES

1 cup Loeb's Prepared Mix
1 egg
1 tablespoon butter
8 quarter-grain saccharin tab-
lets (Loeb's or 6 drops of Loeb's Sweetener)
1 cup water

Dissolve saccharin in water. Stir egg and water together. Sift prepared mix. Stir liquid into the mix. Lightly butter pan or griddle. Spoon batter onto hot griddle, turning over when lightly browned. Serve with Loeb's Maple Mix.

Makes 8 griddle cakes. 56 calories per pancake.

TABLES OF WEIGHTS AND MEASURES

Dash (dry) ....less than ⅛ teaspoon
Dash (liquid) ....a few drops
3 teaspoons ....1 tablespoon
2 liquid tablespoons ....1 ounce
4 tablespoons ....¼ cup
1 cup ....½ pint
1 cup ....8 ounces
2 cups ....1 pint
2 pints ....1 quart
1 quart ....4 cups
4 quarts ....1 gallon
8 quarts ....1 peck
4 pecks ....1 bushel
1 pound ....16 ounces
4 cups flour ....1 pound
2 cups granulated sugar ....1 pound
2 cups solid meat ....1 pound
5 whole eggs ....1 pound
2 tablespoons butter ....1 ounce
½ cup butter ....¼ pound
2 cups butter ....1 pound

CALORIE CHARTS

Milk, Cream, Cheese; Related
Products

Milk, cow's:		
Fluid, whole	1 cup	165
Fluid, non-fat (skim)	1 cup	90
Buttermilk, cultured, from skim milk	1 cup	90
Evaporated, unsweetened, undiluted	1 cup	345
Condensed, sweetened, undiluted	1 cup	985
Dry, whole	1 cup	515
Dry, non-fat	1 cup	290
Milk, goat's:		
Fluid, whole	1 cup	165
Cream:		
Half-and-half (milk and cream)	1 cup	330
	1 tablespoon	20
Light, table or coffee	1 cup	525
	1 tablespoon	35
Whipping, unwhipped (volume about double when whipped):		
Medium	1 cup	745
	1 tablespoon	45

*Number
of
calories*

Heavy	1 cup	860
	1 tablespoon	55
Cheese:		
Blue Mold (Roquefort type)	1 ounce	105
Cheddar or American:		
Ungrated	1-inch cube	70
Grated	1 cup	455
	1 tablespoon	30
Cheddar, process	1 ounce	105
Cheese foods, Cheddar	1 ounce	95
Cottage cheese, from skim milk:		
Creamed	1 cup	240
	1 ounce	30
Uncreamed	1 cup	195
	1 ounce	25
Cream cheese	1 ounce	105
	1 tablespoon	55
Swiss	1 ounce	105
Milk beverages:		
Chocolate-flavored milk drink	1 cup	190
Cocoa	1 cup	235
Malted milk	1 cup	280
Milk desserts:		
Cornstarch pudding, plain	1 cup	275
Custard, baked	1 cup	285
Ice Cream, plain, factory packed:		
Container	1 slice	145
Container	3½ fluid ounces	130
Iced milk	8 fluid ounces	295
⅛ of a quart	1 cup	285

Yoghurt, from partially
    skimmed milk   1 cup 120
Eggs

Eggs, large, 24 ounces per
dozen:
    Raw:
        Whole, without shell   1 egg 80
        White of egg   1 white 15
        Yolk of egg   1 yolk 60
    Cooked:
        Boiled, shell removed   1 egg 80
        Scrambled, with milk
        and fat   1 egg 110

*Meat, Poultry, Fish, Shellfish;
Related Products*

Bacon, broiled or fried crisp   2 slices 95
Beef, trimmed to retail basis,
    cooked:
    Cuts braised, simmered, or
        pot-roasted:
        Lean and fat   3 ounces 245
        Lean only   2.5 ounces 140
    Hamburger, broiled:
        Market ground   3 ounces 245
        Ground lean   3 ounces 185
    Roast, oven-cooked, no
        liquid added:
        Relatively fat, such as
            rib:
            Lean and fat   3 ounces 390
            Lean only   1.8 ounces 120

Relatively lean, such as round:		
Lean and fat	3 ounces	220
Lean only	2.5 ounces	130
Steak, broiled:		
Relatively fat, such as sirloin		
Lean and fat	3 ounces	330
Lean only	2 ounces	115
Relatively lean, such as round:		
Lean and fat	3 ounces	220
Lean only	2.4 ounces	130
Beef, canned:		
Corned beef	3 ounces	180
Corned beef hash	3 ounces	120
Beef, dried or chipped	2 ounces	115
Beef potpie, baked: Individual pie,		
4½-inch diameter, weight before baking about 8 ounces	1 pie	460
Chicken, cooked:		
Flesh and skin, broiled	3 ounces, without bone	185
Breast, fried, ½ breast:		
With bone	3.3 ounces	215
Flesh and skin only	2.8 ounces	215
Leg, fried (thigh and drumstick):		
With bone	4.3 ounces	245
Flesh and skin only	3.1 ounces	245
Chicken, canned, boneless	3 ounces	170
Chicken potpie: See Poultry potpie		

Calorie Charts

Chile con carne, canned:		
With beans	1 cup	335
Without beans	1 cup	510
Heart, beef, trimmed of fat,		
braised	3 ounces	160
Lamb, trimmed to retail basis,		
cooked:		
Chop, thick, with bone,		
broiled	1 chop, 4.8 ounces	405
Lean and fat	4 ounces	405
Lean only	2.6 ounces	140
Leg, roasted:		
Lean and fat	3 ounces	235
Lean only	2.5 ounces	130
Shoulder, roasted:		
Lean and fat	3 ounces	285
Lean only	2 ounces	130
Liver, beef, fried	2 ounces	120
Pork, cured, cooked:		
Ham, smoked, lean and fat	3 ounces	290
Luncheon meat:		
Cooked ham, sliced	2 ounces	170
Canned, spiced or		
unspiced	2 ounces	165
Pork, fresh, trimmed to retail		
basis, cooked:		
Chop, thick, with bone	1 chop, 3.5 ounces	260
Lean and fat	2.3 ounces	260
Lean only	1.7 ounces	130
Roast, oven-cooked, no		
liquid added:		
Lean and fat	3 ounces	310
Lean only	2.4 ounces	175

Cuts simmered:		
Lean and fat	3 ounces	320
Lean only	2.2 ounces	135
Poultry potpie (chicken or turkey):		
Individual pie, 4¼-inch diameter, about 8 ounces	1 pie	485
Sausage:		
Bologna, slice, 4.1 by 0.1 inch	8 slices	690
Frankfurter, cooked	1 frankfurter	155
Pork, bulk, canned	4 ounces	340
Tongue, beef, simmered	3 ounces	205
Turkey potpie: See Poultry potpie		
Veal, cooked:		
Cutlet, broiled	3 ounces, without bone	185
Roast, medium fat, medium done:		
Lean and fat	3 ounces	305
Fish and shellfish:		
Bluefish, baked or broiled	3 ounces	135
Clams:		
Raw, meat only	3 ounces	70
Canned, solids and liquid	3 ounces	45
Crabmeat, canned or cooked	3 ounces	90
Fishsticks, breaded, cooked, frozen stick, 3.8 by 1.0 by 0.5 inch	10 sticks or 8 ounce package	400
Haddock, fried	3 ounces	135

Mackerel:
  Broiled, Atlantic   3 ounces 200
  Canned, Pacific, solids
    and liquid   3 ounces 155
Ocean perch, breaded (egg
  and breadcrumbs) fried   3 ounces 195
Oysters, meat only: raw,
  13-19 medium selects   1 cup 160
Oyster stew, 1 part oysters
  to 3 parts milk by vol-
  ume, 3-4 oysters   1 cup 200
Salmon, pink, canned   3 ounces 120
Sardines, Atlantic type,
  canned in oil, drained
  solids   3 ounces 180
Shad, baked   3 ounces 170
Shrimp, canned, meat only 3 ounces 110
Swordfish, broiled with
  butter or margarine   3 ounces 150
Tuna, canned in oil,
  drained solids   3 ounces 170

*Mature Dry Beans and Peas,
Nuts, Peanuts; Related Products*

Almonds, shelled   1 cup 850
Beans, dry:
  Common varieties, such as
  Great Northern, navy, and
  others, canned:
  Red   1 cup 230
  White, with tomato or
    molasses:
    With pork   1 cup 330
    Without pork   1 cup 315

Lima, cooked	1 cup	260
Brazil nuts, broken pieces	1 cup	905
Cashew nuts, roasted	1 cup	770
Coconut:		
Fresh, shredded	1 cup	330
Dried, shredded, sweetened	1 cup	345
Cowpeas or blackeye peas, dry, cooked	1 cup	190
Peanuts, roasted, shelled:		
Halves	1 cup	840
Chopped	1 tablespoon	50
Peanut butter	1 tablespoon	90
Peas, split, dry, cooked	1 cup	290
Pecans:		
Halves	1 cup	740
Chopped	1 tablespoon	50
Walnuts, shelled:		
Black or native, chopped	1 cup	790
English or Persian:		
Halves	1 cup	650
Chopped	1 tablespoon	50

Vegetables and Vegetable Products

Asparagus:		
Cooked, cut spears	1 cup	35
Canned spears, medium:		
Green	6 spears	20
Bleached	6 spears	20
Beans:		
Lima, immature, cooked	1 cup	150
Snap, green:		
Cooked:		
In a small amount of water, short time	1 cup	25

In large amount of water, long time	1 cup	25
Canned:		
Solids and liquid	1 cup	45
Strained or chopped	1 ounce	5
Bean sprouts: See Sprouts		
Beets, cooked, diced	1 cup	70
Broccoli spears, cooked	1 cup	45
Brussels sprouts, cooked	1 cup	60
Cabbage:		
Raw:		
Finely shredded	1 cup	25
Coleslaw	1 cup	100
Cooked:		
In small amount of water, short time	1 cup	40
In large amount of water, long time	1 cup	40
Cabbage, celery or Chinese:		
Raw, leaves and stem, 1-inch pieces	1 cup	15
Cooked	1 cup	25
Carrots:		
Raw:		
Whole, 5½ by 1 inch	1 carrot	20
Grated	1 cup	45
Cooked, diced	1 cup	45
Canned, strained or chopped	1 ounce	5
Cauliflower, cooked, flowerbuds	1 cup	30
Celery, raw:		
Stalk, large outer, 8 by about 1½ inches at root end	1 stalk	5
Pieces, diced	1 cup	20

Collards, cooked	1 cup	75
Corn, sweet:		
Cooked, ear 5 by 1¾ inches	1 ear	65
Canned, solids and liquid	1 cup	170
Cowpeas, cooked, immature		
seeds	1 cup	150
Cucumbers, 10-ounce, 7½ by		
about 2 inches	1 cucumber	25
Dandelion greens, cooked	1 cup	80
Endive, curly (including		
escarole)	2 ounces	10
Kale, cooked	1 cup	45
Lettuce, headed, raw:		
Head, looseleaf, 4-inch		
diameter	1 head	30
Head, compact, 4¾ inch		
diameter, 1 pound	1 head	70
Leaves	2 large or 4 small	5
Mushrooms, canned, solids and		
liquid	1 cup	30
Mustard greens, cooked	1 cup	30
Okra, cooked, pod 3 by ⅝ inch	8 pods	30
Onions:		
Mature:		
Raw, onion 2½-inch		
diameter	1 onion	50
Cooked	1 cup	80
Young green, small, without		
tops	6 onions	25
Parsley, raw, chopped	1 tablespoon	1
Parsnips, cooked	1 cup	95
Peas, green:		
Cooked	1 cup	110
Canned, solids and liquid	1 cup	170
Canned, strained	1 ounce	10

		Number of calories
Peppers, hot, red, without seeds, dried;		
ground chili powder	1 tablespoon	50
Peppers, sweet:		
Raw, medium, about 6 per pound:		
Green pod without stem and seeds	1 pod	15
Red pod without stem and seeds	1 pod	20
Canned, pimentos, medium	1 pod	10
Potatoes, medium, about 3 per pound:		
Baked, peeled after baking	1 potato	90
Boiled:		
Peeled after boiling	1 potato	105
Peeled before boiling	1 potato	90
French-fried, piece 2 by ½ by ½ inch:		
Cooked in deep fat, ready to eat	10 pieces	155
Frozen, ready to heat for serving	10 pieces	95
Mashed:		
Milk added	1 cup	145
Milk and butter added	1 cup	230
Potato chips, medium, 2-inch diameter	10 chips	110
Pumpkin, canned	1 cup	75
Radishes, raw, small	4 radishes	10
Sauerkraut, canned, drained solids	1 cup	30
Spinach:		
Cooked	1 cup	45

Number of calories

Canned, drained solids	1 cup	45
Canned, drained and creamed	1 ounce	10
Sprouts, raw:		
Mung bean	1 cup	20
Soybean	1 cup	50
Squash:		
Cooked:		
Summer, diced	1 cup	35
Winter, baked, mashed	1 cup	95
Canned, winter, strained or chopped	1 ounce	10
Sweet potatoes:		
Cooked, medium, 5 by 2 inches, weight about 6 ounces:		
Baked, peeled after baking	1 sweet potato	155
Boiled, peeled after boiling	1 sweet potato	170
Candied, $3\frac{1}{2}$ by $2\frac{1}{4}$ inches	1 sweet potato	295
Canned, vacuum or solid pack	1 cup	235
Tomatoes:		
Raw, medium 2 by $2\frac{1}{2}$ inches, about 3 per pound	1 tomato	30
Canned or cooked	1 cup	45
Tomato juice, canned	1 cup	50
Tomato catsup	1 tablespoon	15
Turnips, cooked, diced	1 cup	40
Turnip greens:		
Cooked:		
In small amount of water, short time	1 cup	45

In large amount of water, long time	1 cup	45
Canned, solids and liquid	1 cup	40

Fruits and Fruit Products

Apples, raw, medium, 2½ inch diameter, about 3 per pound	1 apple	70
Apple brown betty	1 cup	350
Apple juice, fresh or canned	1 cup	125
Apple sauce, canned:		
Sweetened	1 cup	185
Unsweetened	1 cup	100
Apricots:		
Raw, about 12 per pound	3 apricots	55
Canned in heavy sirup:		
Halves and sirup	1 cup	220
Halves, medium, and sirup	4 halves, 2 tbs. sirup	105
Dried:		
Uncooked, 40 halves, small	1 cup	390
Cooked, unsweetened, fruit and liquid	1 cup	240
Apricots and apple sauce, canned (strained or chopped)	1 ounce	20
Apricot nectar	1 cup	140
Avocados, raw: California varieties:		
10-ounce avocado, about 3⅓ by 4¼ inches, peeeled, pitted	½ avocado	185
½-inch cubes	1 cup	260

Florida varieties:
    13-ounce avocado, about
    4 by 3 inches, peeled,
    pitted   ½ avocado 160
    ½-inch cubes   1 cup 195
Bananas, raw, 6 by 1½ inches,
    about 3 per pound   1 banana 85
Blackberries, raw   1 cup 85
Blueberries, raw   1 cup 85
Cantaloups, raw, medium, 5-inch
    diameter, about 1⅔ pounds   ½ melon 40
Cherries:
    Raw, sour, sweet, hybrid   1 cup 65
    Canned, red, sour, pitted   1 cup 105
Cranberry juice cocktail, canned   1 cup 140
Cranberry sauce, sweetened,
    canned or cooked   1 cup 550
Dates, "fresh" and dried, pitted,
    cut   1 cup 505
Figs:
    Raw, small, 1½-inch
    diameter, about 12 per
    pound   3 figs 90
    Dried, large, 2 by 1 inch   1 fig 60
Fruit cocktail, canned in heavy
    sirup, solids and liquid   1 cup 195
Grapefruit:
    Raw, medium, 4¼ inch
    diameter, size 64:
      White   ½ grapefruit 50
      Pink or red   ½ grapefruit 55
    Raw sections, white   1 cup 75
    Canned:
      Sirup pack, solids and
      liquid   1 cup 170

Water pack, solids and liquid	1 cup	70
Grapefruit juice:		
Fresh	1 cup	95
Canned:		
Sweetened	1 cup	100
Unsweetened	1 cup	130
Frozen, concentrate, unsweetened:		
Undiluted, can, 6 fluid ounces	1 can	300
Water added	1 cup	100
Frozen, concentrated, sweetened:		
Undiluted, can, 6 fluid ounces	1 can	350
Water added	1 cup	115
Dehydrated:		
Crystals, can, net weight, 4 ounces	1 can	430
Water added	1 can	100
Grapes, raw:		
American type (slip skin), such as Concord, Delaware, Niagara and Scuppernong	1 cup	70
European type (adherent skin), such as Malaga, Muscat, Sultana and Flame Tokay	1 cup	100
Grape juice, bottled	1 cup	165
Lemons, raw, medium, 2-1/5 inch diameter, size 150	1 lemon	20

Lemon juice:		
Fresh	1 cup	60
	1 tablespoon	5
Canned, unsweetened	1 cup	60
Lemonade concentrate, frozen, sweetened:		
Undiluted, can, 6 fluid ounces	1 can	430
Water added	1 cup	110
Lime juice:		
Fresh	1 cup	65
Canned	1 cup	65
Limeade concentrate, frozen, sweetened:		
Undiluted, can, 6 fluid ounces	1 can	405
Water added	1 cup	105
Oranges, raw:		
Navel, California (winter), size 88, 2-4/5-inch diameter	1 orange	60
Other varieties, 3-inch diameter	1 orange	70
Orange juice:		
Fresh:		
California, Valencia, summer	1 cup	120
Florida varieties:		
Early and midseason	1 cup	100
Late season, Valencia	1 cup	110
Canned, unsweetened	1 cup	120
Frozen concentrate:		
Undiluted, can, 6 fluid ounces	1 can	330
Water added	1 cup	110

		Number of calories
Dehydrated:		
Crystals, can, net weight		
4 ounces	1 can	430
Water added	1 cup	115
Orange and grapefruit juice:		
Frozen concentrate:		
Undiluted, can, 6 fluid		
ounces	1 can	330
Water added	1 cup	110
Papayas, raw, ½-inch cubes	1 cup	70
Peaches:		
Raw:		
Whole, medium, 2-inch		
diameter, about 4 per		
pound	1 peach	35
Sliced	1 cup	65
Canned, yellow-fleshed,		
solids and liquid:		
Sirup pack, heavy:		
Halves or slices	1 cup	200
Halves, medium, and		
sirup	2 halves and 2 table-spoons sirup	90
Water pack	1 cup	75
Strained	1 ounce	20
Dried:		
Uncooked	1 cup	420
Cooked, unsweetened, 10-12 halves and 6 tablespoons liquid	1 cup	220
Frozen:		
Carton, 12 ounce	1 carton	265
Can, 16 ounce	1 can	355
Peach nectar, canned	1 cup	115

Pears:
    Raw, 3 by 2½ inch
      diameter .... 1 pear 100
    Canned, solids and liquid:
      Sirup pack, heavy:
        Halves or slices .... 1 cup 195
        Halves, medium, and
          sirup .... 2 halves and 2 table-
               spoons sirup 90
        Water pack .... 1 cup 80
        Strained .... 1 ounce 15
Pear Nectar, canned .... 1 cup 130
Persimmons, Japanese or kaki,
    raw, seedless, 2½-inch
    diameter .... 1 persimmon 75
Pineapple:
    Raw, diced .... 1 cup 75
    Canned, sirup pack, solids
      and liquid:
      Crushed .... 1 cup 205
      Sliced, slices and juice ...... 2 small or 1 large, and
                 2 tablespoons
                 juice 95
Pineapple juice, canned .... 1 cup 120
Plums, all except prunes:
    Raw, 2-inch diameter, about
      2 ounces .... 1 plum 30
    Canned, sirup pack (Italian
      prunes) :
      Plums and juice .... 1 cup 185
      Plums (without pits) and
        juice .... 3 plums and 2 table-
               spoons juice 90

Prunes, dried:
  Medium, 50-60 per pound:
    Uncooked .... 4 prunes 70
    Cooked, unsweetened, 17-
      18 prunes and ⅓ cup
      liquid .... 1 cup 305
    Canned, strained .... 1 ounce 25
Prune juice, canned .... 1 cup 170
Raisins, dried .... 1 cup 460
Raspberries, red:
  Raw .... 1 cup 70
  Frozen, 10-ounce carton .... 1 carton 280
Rhubarb, cooked, sugar added ... 1 cup 385
Strawberries:
  Raw, capped .... 1 cup 55
  Frozen, 10-ounce carton .... 1 carton 300
  Frozen, 16-ounce can .... 1 can 485
Tangerines, raw, medium, 2½-
  inch diameter, about 4 per
  pound .... 1 tangerine 40
Tangerine juice:
  Canned, unsweetened .... 1 cup 105
  Frozen concentrate:
    Undiluted, can, 6 fluid
      ounces .... 1 can 340
    Water added .... 1 cup 115
Watermelon, raw, wedge, 4 by 8
  inches, ... 1 wedge 120

Grain Products

Barley, pearled, light, uncooked ... 1 cup 710
Biscuits, baking powder, with
  enriched flour, 2½-inch
  diameter .... 1 biscuit 130

Bran flakes (40 per cent bran) with added thiamine	1 ounce	85
Breads:		
Boston brown bread, made with degermed cornmeal, slice 3 by ¾-inch	1 slice	100
Cracked-wheat bread:		
Loaf, 1-pound, 20 slices	1 loaf	1190
Slice	1 slice	60
French or Vienna bread:		
Enriched, 1 pound loaf	1 loaf	1315
Unenriched 1 pound loaf	1 loaf	1315
Italian bread:		
Enriched, 1-pound loaf	1 loaf	1250
Unenriched, 1-pound loaf	1 loaf	1250
Raisin bread:		
Loaf, 1 pound, 20 slices	1 loaf	1190
Slice	1 slice	60
Rye bread:		
American, light (⅓ rye, ⅔ wheat) : Loaf, 1-pound, 20 slices	1 loaf	1100
Slice	1 slice	55
Pumpernickel, dark, loaf, 1-pound	1 loaf	1115
White bread, enriched 1 to 2 per cent non-fat dry milk:		
Loaf, 1-pound, 20 slices	1 loaf	1225
Slice	1 slice	60
White bread, unenriched: 1 to 2 per cent non-fat dry milk:		
Loaf, 1-pound, 20 slices	1 loaf	1225
Slice	1 slice	60

		Number of calories
Wholewheat, graham, entire-wheat bread:		
Loaf, 1-pound, 20 slices	1 loaf	1105
Slice	1 slice	55
Breadcrumbs, dry grated	1 cup	345
Cakes:		
Angel food cake; sector, 2-inch (1/12 of 8-inch diameter cake)	1 slice	110
Chocolate cake, fudge icing; sector, 2-inch (1/16 of 10-inch diameter layer cake)	1 slice	420
Fruitcake, dark; piece, 2 by 2 by ½ inch	1 piece	105
Gingerbread; piece, 2 by 2 by 2 inches	1 piece	180
Plain cake and cupcakes, without icing:		
Piece, 3 by 2 by 1½ inches	1 piece	180
Cupcake, 2¾-inch diameter	1 cupcake	130
Plain cake and cupcakes, with icing:		
Sector, 2-inch (1/16 of 10-inch layer cake)	1 slice	320
Cupcake, 2¾ inch diameter	1 cupcake	160
Pound cake; slice, 2¾ by 4 by ⅝ inch	1 slice	130
Sponge cake; sector, 2-inch (1/12 of 8-inch diameter cake)	1 slice	115
Cookies:		
Plain and assorted, 3-inch diameter	1 cookie	110
Fig bars, small	1 fig bar	55

*Number
of
calories*

Corn-cereal mixture (mainly de-germed cornmeal), puffed, with added thiamine, niacin, and iron:	1 ounce	115
Cornflakes, with added thiamine, niacin, and iron:		
Plain	1 ounce	110
Presweetened	1 ounce	110
Corn grits, white, degermed, cooked:		
Enriched	1 cup	120
Unenriched	1 cup	120
Cornmeal, white or yellow, dry:		
Whole ground	1 cup	420
Degermed, enriched	1 cup	525
Corn muffins, made with enriched, degermed cornmeal; muffin, 2¾-inch diameter	1 muffin	155
Corn, puffed, presweetened, with added thiamine, riboflavin, niacin, and iron	1 ounce	110
Corn and soy shreds with added thiamine and niacin	1 ounce	100
Crackers:		
Graham	4 small or 2 medium	55
Saltines, 2 inches square	2 crackers	35
Soda, plain:		
Cracker, 2½ inches square	2 crackers	45
Oyster crackers	10 crackers	45
Cracker meal	1 tablespoon	45
Doughnuts, cake type	1 doughnut	135
Farina, cooked	1 cup	105
Macaroni, cooked	1 cup	155
Macaroni, enriched, and cheese, baked	1 cup	475

Muffins, with enriched white flour; 2¾-inch diameter	1 muffin	135
Noodles (egg noodles), cooked	1 cup	200
Oat-cereal mixture, mainly oats, with added B-vitamins and minerals	1 ounce	115
Oatmeal or rolled oats, regular or quick-cooking, cooked	1 cup	150
Pancakes (griddlecakes), 4-inch diameter:		
Wheat, enriched flour (home recipe)	1 cake	60
Buckwheat (buckwheat pancake mix)	1 cake	45
Piecrust, plain, baked:		
Lower crust, 9-inch shell	1 crust	655
Double crust, 9-inch pie	1 double crust	1315
Pies: sector, 4-inch, 1/7 of 9-inch pie		
Apple	1 sector	330
Cherry	1 sector	340
Custard	1 sector	265
Lemon meringue	1 sector	300
Mince	1 sector	340
Pumpkin	1 sector	265
Pizza (cheese), 5½ inch sector ⅛ of 14-inch diameter pie	1 sector	180
Popcorn, popped	1 cup	55
Pretzels, small stick	5 sticks	20
Rice, cooked:		
Parboiled	1 cup	205
White	1 cup	200
Rice, puffed, with added thiamine, niacin, and iron	1 cup	55

Rice flakes, with added thiamane and niacin	1 cup	115
Rolls:		
Plain, pan (12 per 16 ounces)	1 roll	115
Hard, round (12 per 22 ounces)	1 roll	160
Sweet, pan (12 per 18 ounces)	1 roll	135
Rye wafers, 1⅞ inch by 3½ inches	2 wafers	45
Spaghetti, cooked until tender	1 cup	155
Spaghetti with meat sauce	1 cup	285
Spaghetti in tomato sauce with cheese	1 cup	210
Waffles, with enriched flour, ½ by 4½ by 5½ inches	1 waffle	240
Wheat, puffed:		
With added thiamine, niacin, and iron	1 ounce	100
With added thiamine and niacin; presweetened	1 ounce	105
Wheat, rolled; cooked	1 cup	175
Wheat, shredded, plain	1 ounce	100
Wheat and malted barley cereal, with added thiamine, niacin, and iron	1 ounce	105
Wheat flours:		
Whole wheat, from hard wheats, stirred	1 cup	400
All purpose or family flour:	1 cup	400
Self-rising flour	1 cup	385
Wheat germ, stirred	1 cup	245

		Number of calories
Fats, Oils		
Butter, 4 sticks per pound:		
Sticks, 2	1 cup	1605
Stick, 1/8	1 tablespoon	100
Pat or square	1 pat	50
Fats, cooking:		
Lard	1 cup	1985
	1 tablespoon	135
Vegetable fats	1 cup	1770
	1 tablespoon	110
Margarine, 4 sticks per pound:		
Sticks, 2	1 cup	1615
Stick, 1/8	1 tablespoon	100
Pat or square	1 pat	50
Oils, salad or cooking		
Corn	1 tablespoon	125
Cottonseed	1 tablespoon	125
Olive	1 tablespoon	125
Soybean	1 tablespoon	125
Salad dressings:		
Blue cheese	1 tablespoon	90
Commercial, plain; mayonnaise type	1 tablespoon	60
French	1 tablespoon	60
Home cooked, boiled	1 tablespoon	30
Mayonnaise	1 tablespoon	110
Thousand Island	1 tablespoon	75

Sugars, Sweets

Candy:		
Caramels	1 ounce	120
Chocolate, sweetened, milk	1 ounce	145
Fudge, plain	1 ounce	115
Hard candy	1 ounce	110
Marshmallow	1 ounce	90
Chocolate sirup	1 tablespoon	40

		Number of calories
Honey, strained or extracted	1 tablespoon	60
Jams, marmalades, preserves	1 tablespoon	55
Jellies	1 tablespoon	50
Molasses, cane:		
Light (first extraction)	1 tablespoon	50
Blackstrap (third extraction)	1 tablespoon	45
Sirup, table blends	1 tablespoon	55
Sugar:		
Granulated, cane or beet	1 cup	770
	1 tablespoon	50
Lump, 1⅛ by ⅝ by ⅛ inch	1 lump	25
Powdered, stirred before measuring	1 cup	495
	1 tablespoon	30
Brown, firm packed	1 cup	815
	1 tablespoon	50

Miscellaneous Items

Beer	1 cup	114
Beverages, carbonated:		
Ginger ale	1 cup	80
Cola type	1 cup	105
Bouillon cube, ⅝ inch	1 cube	2
Chili powder: See Vegetables, Peppers		
Chili sauce (mainly tomatoes)	1 tablespoon	15
Chocolate:		
Bitter or unsweetened	1 ounce	145
Sweetened	1 ounce	135
Cider: See Fruit, Applejuice		
Gelatin, dry:		
Plain	1 tablespoon	35
Dessert powder, 3-ounce package	½ cup	325

Gelatin dessert, ready-to-eat:
    Plain .... 1 cup 155
    With fruit .... 1 cup 170
Olives, pickled:
    Green .... 12 extra large 65
    Ripe .... 12 extra large 85
Pickles, cucumber:
    Dill, large, 4 by 1¾ inches ...... 1 pickle 15
    Sweet, 2¾ by ¾ inch .... 1 pickle 20
Popcorn: See Grain products
Sherbet, factory packed .... 1 cup 235
Soups, canned; ready-to-serve:
    Bean .... 1 cup 190
    Beef .... 1 cup 100
    Bouillon, broth, consommé ...... 1 cup 10
    Chicken .... 1 cup 75
    Clam chowder .... 1 cup 85
    Cream soup (asparagus,
      celery, mushroom) .... 1 cup 200
    Noodle, rice, barley .... 1 cup 115
    Pea .... 1 cup 140
    Tomato .... 1 cup 90
    Vegetable .... 1 cup 80
Starch, pure, including arrow-
    root, corn, etc. .... 1 cup 465
                         1 tablespoon 30
Tapioca, quick-cooking, granu-
    lated dry; stirred before
    measuring .... 1 cup 545
Vinegar .... 1 tablespoon 2
White sauce, medium .... 1 cup 430
Yeast:
    Baker's:
    Compressed .... 1 ounce 25
    Dry active .... 1 ounce 80

INDEX OF RECIPES